Christian Leadership i

by David O'Malley SDB

Graphics by Val O'Brien

Credits

Bible selections are from the New Revised Standard Version of the Bible, © 1989 by the Division of Christian Education of the National Council of the Churches of Christ in the USA. Used by permission. All rights reserved. Spirituality and Spiritual Development in Youth Work , The National Youth Agency 2005, used by permission from the National Youth Agency. The Spirit of the Child, Hay and Nye, used by permission of Jessica Kingsley Publishers 2006. The Learning Age, used by permission of HMSO. Handbook for the Inspection of Schools 1994, used by permission of the HMSO. Spiritual and Moral Development , 1993, 1995 used with permission from the National Curriculum Council. Lumen Gentium, Pope Paul VI 1964, with permission from the Vatican.

ISBN 978-0-9548388-9-8

© Don Bosco Publications 2007
Thornleigh House
Sharples Park
BOLTON BL1 6PQ
www.don-bosco-publications.co.uk

CONTENTS

INTRODUCTION

I've found that God likes dressing up
Likes playing hide and seek
Especially when I've work to do
And timetables to keep
I've got so many plans
He could help get off the ground
But God's not around

At least he's not where I can see Him
Or feel he's on my side
He's not in all the plans I've made
To bolster up my pride
But in the interruptions
Through which I ride roughshod
There is God

So I missed God in the sunshine
That warmed my hands and face
Missed God in the youngster
That I sent off in disgrace
Missed God in the woman
Who would not let me speak
I think I'll have to work some more
At playing hide and seek

These words attempt to capture something of the dilemma of leaders in Christian communities; to be involved with delivery of plans, targets and budgets: yet be sensitive to the hidden presence of God in all that happens. This short book aims to help leaders strengthen their awareness of the spiritual dimension of leadership in school and youth groups by looking at the way gospel patterns can emerge through the service of authority in a Christian community.

The vocational dimension of carrying responsibility is the main focus of this book. That spiritual thread is traced in the vagaries of planning and of confronting colleagues, in building teams and recognising the spiritual patterns unfolding in ordinary events. Touching that deeper stream of consciousness in leadership gives energy and increased stamina in the often hidden burden of leadership. Each chapter explores one area of leadership experience and ends with a personal reflection for the reader.

The book will be helpful for those involved in leadership in schools, including governors and heads of department. It will also support the more informal work of youth leaders and catechists in church settings. The book concludes with a list of resources and short prayers specifically for those involved in school and youth leadership. These can be used personally by leaders or may form the basis of a reflection for the teams they lead. In a society that seems to be either fanatic or dismissive about God, this book may help leaders to find a map and compass to a deeper sense of the spirit in the service of young people.

CHAPTER 1

SPIRITUALITY – EDUCATION – RELIGION

Spirituality, at its most basic level, is whatever gets a person out of bed in the morning. As it becomes more *focused* it opens up levels of personal awareness that take an individual into mystery, awe and wonder at their world and their own experience. At that stage, spirituality is rather vague and easily marginalised both by the individual and the culture in which they live. Spirituality takes on a specific shape in the balanced traditions of the world religions. Through their creeds, morality and sense of community these spiritual traditions give meaning, shape and value to individuals and to a culture.

Many people say they are *spiritual but not religious.* They have a general sense of believing, without any sense of belonging to a group or a church. Our culture is suspicious of religion, and tries to marginalise its influence on our lives. Today's culture tends to privatise it into a subjective world, where it loses any significance for decision-making in practical settings. This is separating the engine from its fuel, where religion is the engine and spirituality is the fuel. Neither can function alone. The fuel, spread out in individual pools, simply evaporates into the atmosphere. Without the energy of spirituality, religion rusts away. No longer an engine of change, it fades into a curious museum piece.

This separation and confusion between spirituality and religion is not just academic when we are dealing with young people's need for meaning, morality and values. It will affect everything we do. The way we, as adults, plan, relate, discipline and evaluate will speak of the value we put on the inner life of young people. The way we use the language of religion will help or hinder young people's progression to a more integrated and influential faith life. The readiness to adopt not just the language of faith but the practical values it carries can make a huge impact on the inner spiritual strength of young people, as they emerge from schools and projects.

The values carried in the prayer *Our Father*, for example, set an agenda that could inform all relationships, mission statements and discipline policies in our work with young people. The values built into the beatitudes from the fifth chapter of Matthew's gospel still have a huge amount to say about the way adults and young people can work together, in educational settings.

This book is an attempt to make connections between the Christian tradition and the best practice that operates in education. The links are not to be seen as a superficial *spot the connections* exercise. Instead they are an unpacking of the Christian values already embedded deep in our own culture. The good practice proposed by educators and organisations such as OFSTED (Office for Standards in Education) are often the anonymous expressions of Christian values that do need to be recognised. In recognising the religious roots of much good practice, the energy of the spirituality and religious traditions can be brought together; leading us to a more focused and holistic experience of education; leading us to fullness of life.

Christian Spirituality

Whilst spirituality is universal and elusively present in each person, it becomes focused and tangible in the language and symbols of major world religions. That focus helps to create a community with common values and it can give shape and direction to the school community or the youth project in which it operates. This collection of values, traditions and shared stories is part of the ethos that makes communities work well and endure through time.

In Christian settings, the vague notion of spirituality becomes clearer. It takes on a shape that is recognisable and opens up a source of meaning and mystery in at least four ways:

1. General spirituality becomes gospel focused.

2. The gospel offers symbols and stories that respect and value the inner world of each person.

3. The gospel offers a clear set of values based on the spiritual nature of each person as belonging to one another in the mystery of God.

4. The gospel-based spirituality offers a world-wide tradition that can offer ongoing spiritual support to young people through the whole of their lives.

In some Christian traditions the emphasis is more on word, rather than on symbols and sacraments. In other traditions the place of sacraments is seen as central. Christian spirituality is built on the lived experience that God became a human being. Therefore God is to be discovered within human experience, in what happens to us and how we cope with life. This earthy approach to spirituality in the muddles and emotions of ordinary life is sometimes called *Incarnational Spirituality*, in contrast to the *Other-Worldly Spirituality* of some faith expressions.

Christian spirituality is therefore a way of opening up our experience; finding meaning and mystery in the ordinary joys and challenges of each day. It is a gift to be offered to young people through a lived experience. It is not enough to talk about Christian spirituality; it must be a lived experience. For example, if the adults working with young people are ready to apologise when they make mistakes, the words they say about Christian forgiveness are more likely to touch hearts and strengthen community. Mission statements do not create a spirituality. Instead it is the thousands of hidden choices that individuals make in an ordinary day that really count. Engaging that inner life, in order to focus it positively, is the task of spirituality in schools and youth settings. It is not an optional extra; it is the one thing that will endure.

Christianity is an optimistic spirituality that emphasises the persistence of life and goodness, despite setbacks. It gives a huge dignity to the individuals and their ability to touch God. It sees all of creation as good, but in need of care. It sees each individual as capable of an eternal relationship with God.

Spirituality and Education

Spirituality is an elusive concept, partly because it is personal and resists analysis, but also because it refers to something that is unknowable in the conventional sense. It deals with faith, meaning and the inner life. A youth-work publication tries to capture the nature of spirituality by drawing up a list rather than a definition:

Spirituality is about the other, either the other in terms of a God or a transcendent being, or the other in terms of being different to the more mundane areas of life.

Spirituality is not something separate from life but flows through life almost as a different but essential dimension.

Spirituality is being squeezed out of people's experience because of the present cultural expectation of achieving fulfilment through *having* rather than *being*.

Spirituality is connected with crises and peak experiences in one's life.

Spirituality is something to do with relationship and connection – both with people and in community, and with the environment and the world.

Spirituality is an internal sense of meaning and story, a deep understanding of *Who I am and my place here*[1]

The subtle nature of spirituality comes through clearly in the listing above. What also emerges is an awareness that certain aspects of our culture can be toxic to the inner spiritual life of young people and adults alike. In the listing above, consumerism, having rather than being, is seen as a value that undermines spirituality in the culture. When Jesus asks people not to store up treasure, the same awareness is at work. The gospel roots of a Christian culture emerge from the words of an apparently secular document and invite a more holistic approach. David Hay, reflecting on the way culture impacts on the spirituality of young people has this to say:

> **The adult world into which our children are inducted is more often than not destructive of their spirituality. Children emerge from infancy with a simplicity that is richly open to experience, only to close off their awareness as they become street-wise.**[2]

Hay suggests that there is a culturally-constructed forgetfulness about the value of the *spiritual* in Britain at present. The inner life of children is effectively ignored in planning and given little emphasis in practice; yet there is a recognition that it is essential to the life of society. Hay has suggested that much of the change in education over recent years has been urged on by an awareness of a deep spiritual and moral vacuum in society. David Blunkett, commenting on this need wrote:

> **As well as securing our economic future, learning has a wider contribution. It helps make ours a civilized society, develops a spiritual side of our lives and promotes active citizenship. Learning enables people to play a full part in their community. It strengthens the family, the neighbourhood and consequently the nation.**[3]

This ideal view of education is repeated in many OFSTED (Office for Standards in Education) definitions. The one below is particularly eloquent about the ways and means of developing the spiritual life of young people. The 1994 inspection handbook attempted a definition of spiritual development:

---

1   The National Youth Agency *Spirituality and Spiritual Development in Youth Work* 2005

2   Hay and Nye *The Spirit of the Child* page 33 Jessica Kingsley Publishers 2006

3   *The Learning Age* HMSO 1998

Spiritual development relates to that aspect of inner life through which pupils acquire insights into their personal experience which are of enduring worth. It is characterised by reflection, the attribution of meaning to experience, valuing a non-material dimension to life and intimations of an enduring reality. Spiritual is not synonymous with religious; all areas of the curriculum may contribute to pupils' spiritual development.[4]

Another educational document that became a key text for the evaluation of the spiritual and moral dimension drew up a similar kind of listing to that from the National Youth Agency. It included

Beliefs
Sense of awe, wonder and mystery
Feelings of transcendence
The search for meaning and purpose
Self knowledge
Relationships
Creativity
Feelings and emotions[5]

This expression of spiritual value may come as a surprise to those who have experienced an OFSTED (Office for Standards in Education) inspection either in youth work or school settings. In those events there is very little space for the valuing of a non-material dimension, where evidence is by definition unavailable in measurable forms. By recognising only what can be measured and evidenced, OFSTED tends to undermine its own desire to enhance the spiritual dimension. Statements of spiritual value are placed among the general introductions to documents and rarely receive recognition or value at the time of inspection. If, as a society, we only value what we can measure, then we have condemned ourselves to superficial living. We have separated individuals and institutions from the deeper spiritual energy they need to create community and meaning.

The implications of all this for leadership in youth work and schooling are far reaching. In order to be spiritual in today's climate it is necessary to be counter-cultural. There is a need to balance the emphasis on measurability

---

4   *Handbook for the Inspection of Schools.* Part 4. Inspection Schedule Guidance. Consolidated Edition, 1994. HMSO Page 86.

5   National Curriculum Council *Spiritual and Moral Development* 1993 republished 1995

and performance with an emphasis on inner life, wonder and the immeasurable mystery that lies at the heart of each person. In that depth lies the energy to raise performance and hit targets, without damaging the spirit of the young people with whom we work.

Leadership therefore does not mean simply meeting the targets proposed by the government. It means calling young people to life, to mystery, to a relationship and to an ongoing faith journey. In engaging in this task the leader finds the heart and the energy to bear the rawness and inconsistency of young people and to go the extra mile in their service. Leaders find a vocation; becoming not just instructors, but guides and mentors for young people and for the staff whom they lead.

Questions

Where do you see the spiritual dimension at work in your present role?

Who are the spiritual people in your team and how have you recognised that dimension in their work?

Where is the spiritual life of young people and staff most likely to be overlooked in your present way of working?

How has the spiritual dimension of your own life developed through work with young people and with adults?

Reflection

Lord, open my eyes to your presence
Tugging me towards the eternal
In everyday routines and timetables.
Give me eyes to see
That the sacred lies within the secular
Just as treasure is buried in the field of life.

Help me to find that treasure
Buried in the hearts of colleagues and the young.
May I make time to reflect
On the deeper meaning of what I see each day.
On corridors, in meetings and in conflict
Open my eyes to the fleeting flashes
Of your treasured life living in people.

May your spirit open me up
To new ways of seeing and deeper ways of working
So that I might be a faithful guide,
A wise worker in this educating community.
Give me the insight that will make me into
A conscious carrier of your spirit,
A sign and a bearer of your own loving kindness.

CHAPTER 2

LEADERSHIP AS VOCATION

The idea of vocation lies at the heart of Christian spirituality. A vocation is first and foremost a relationship. Each person is called to engage with the mystery of life and recognise the *otherness* that lies at the heart of each individual. It was that awareness of mystery and meaning that Jesus was able to name as *Father*, a relationship that was to prove stronger than death. The notion of vocation is not just a specific call to roles in the Church but something that happens to everyone who has ears to hear. Neither is a vocation necessarily a *churchy* experience. I remember speaking to a young man who told me that Jesus had appeared on the bonnet of his car and told him to become a priest. Such experiences should generally lead to a visit to the doctor rather than to a priest. The usual mode of vocational discernment demands more earthy explorations into the mystery of each person's story and the story of the culture in which they live. As a leader in a Christian community, it is important to recognise one's own sense of vocation as that inner and urgent drive to make a difference in the lives of others.

Like all relationships, a vocation is not just a general call to a career. We are called as we are, each with our own history, strengths and weaknesses, into a relationship and a partnership with what is deepest in life. The style we adopt, the concerns and priorities that energise us and the parts of leadership that expose our weakness will all depend on our personal story and the demands made upon us by others. It is we who are called to work with the young, through our strengths, through our weaknesses and through our own story. Life calls us to education and the God of life supports us as we follow that call.

In the Christian tradition Baptism is the sacrament of vocation; the point at which we recognise a relationship with God and promise to put it at the centre of our living. Not all leaders who work in Christian communities are baptised but all such leaders are called to awaken that relationship in some way in each young person. The sacrament expresses this relationship in three ways: as priest, as prophet and as king. Each word can help to enlighten how the vocation of leadership takes on a particular shape in a Christian community and in a specific person.

The Leader as Priest

A priest is someone who brings God's presence to mind through words and actions. A priest reminds people of a deeper reality at work in the ordinary moments of life. In a similar way each leader in a Christian community is called to be a sign and bearer of God's love, especially for young people. Leadership is a spiritual role. That spiritual dimension demands time for reflection, self-knowledge, and a deeper level of awareness of mystery in everyday patterns. Unless a leader takes time to reflect spiritually they may miss the energy and enthusiasm behind a colleague's criticism. They might misinterpret the significance of a pupil's gratitude or resist change for selfish motives.

Leaders have a priestly role because they are asked to work on the bigger picture of the Christian community and not just on the details. They are asked to offer guidance within the spirit and ethos of that community. At times they will be asked to defend and develop the sacred moments and values that mark out the tradition in which they work. Leaders also share the priestly role of baptised Christians by blessing and encouraging what makes for life and growth among young people and colleagues alike. They are mystic and intuitive; seeing beneath the surface of routines, to the values and the energy that binds the community to spiritual roots.

The Leader as Prophet

In the baptismal service a Christian is called to be a prophet; one who will speak the truth and challenge what works against the spirit of the gospel. This aspect of leadership is essential if a community is to be true to its gospel inspiration. Prophets are not usually popular people; they say things that others don't want to hear. They say what they see. The prophet will see reality through the values of the gospel and notice where the compromises happen and where other values are undermining the gospel. The prophetic leader will be concerned with justice for colleagues and young people alike. They will focus on those most at risk in the community and try to ease their burden. In leadership the values of consistency and fairness will predominate and they will be ready to admit their own failures when they happen.

Prophets are restless leaders because nothing is ever perfect. They will tend to champion specific causes and be very focused through to a conclusion. In discipline issues they can tend to let their anger show, but be acutely aware of the need for reconciliation and closure after an incident. They will want to adapt policies and plans to the spiritual needs and the rights of the community and each individual. They are the watchful figures in any team; challengers of fearful compromises, but they are vital to Christian leadership.

The Leader as King

At the baptismal service the vocation of a Christian is also seen as a sharing of the kingship of Christ. The Christian accepts a share of responsibility for building and maintaining the kingdom of God; that place where the presence of God is recognised and gospel values lived out. Kingly leaders accept the gift of authority and administration as a way of loving and serving the community to which they belong. When authority is needed they are ready to use it confidently within the spirit of the gospel. When boundaries are needed and sanctions must be imposed kingly leaders are able to do both with reasoned humility. This aspect of leadership identifies them most closely with the groups and individuals within the community. They are keen to consult, to coordinate and to explain rather than rush decisions when haste is not essential.

Kingly leaders value harmony and reason in managing their responsibilities. They know that they have a sacred trust and value the dignity of each person in the community because they are all sons and daughters of God. Kingly leaders recognise that the spiritual has to become real in careful decisions, clear rules and clear relationships. They fulfil their vocation through caring, in being faithful to order and accountability.

The Leadership Vocation rooted in experience

The Christian vocation described as priest, prophet and king will never adequately capture the mystery of an individual's call to leadership in a Christian community. Each calling puts on the flesh and blood of the life story of each person. The way a person's story unfolds will open up a unique sense of calling and relationship to God. That story contains not only the energy to lead well, but also a pathway to personal meaning for the leaders themselves. The call to action in the community and the personal call to meaning, meet in a Christian leader's vocation and give them the task of transforming their outer and inner world.

The calling to leadership comes through ordinary events, accidents, coincidences, gifts, failures and significant relationships. Within each of these situations the mystery of a vocation to leadership can be triggered. Some leaders may feel that they have made a career choice, that they have been motivated simply by ambition and money. In fact, most leaders draw their energy not from salary cheques but from spiritual values. It is only these deeper values that can sustain leaders in their role when faced with aggression, indifference and misunderstanding. Money is insufficient to motivate a leader for long in serving the needs of a community.

To appreciate how deep vocation reaches into life stories two case studies are attached for reflection. They are not extraordinary. This type of personal pattern is repeated in staff settings in many schools and youth projects. They represent the way the spirit works in people to call them to life and to self-sacrifice. It is at this level that the spiritual and moral energy is born that sustains relationships in Christian schools and projects. Leaders who ignore this deeper level of spirituality are likely to find it hard to sustain motivation and energy through change and to bear patiently with the frustration of working with the young. Leaders who do touch this well of experience and bring it to awareness are likely to be calmer under pressure, more inspirational in relationships and open-minded in planning.

Case Study One

Mary has been a teacher for twelve years. She recently applied to be head of year 10 and performed very well at interview. Some of her colleagues told her it wasn't worth taking on the extra hassle for the small increase in salary. At one level Mary knew they were right. She knew it would be hard, that she would be face-to-face with a lot of aggressive adolescents and that some colleagues would use her, to avoid taking responsibility for their own discipline. Yet she still wanted the job, was sure it was right for her now, but didn't really know why.

Having said *Yes*, she sat at home with a glass of wine and thought it through. After some frustrating moments an image of her own form tutor came into her mind. Mr Casey was the kind of teacher she had modelled herself on and much of what he did she found herself doing for her own pupils, with both energy and ease. *Why had he come back into her mind?* She didn't really know. Then she remembered a conversation she had with him after her exams. He had told her she would make a good teacher, that she had the gifts to work with people and that she was a natural. The memory was good, warm and inspiring. So had Mr Casey called her to teach? Or had he just recognised something in her that she couldn't see clearly, even now.

She had been a normal girl at school, did well and joined in most things. School was always important to her. When home life was chaotic she had valued the routine and hopefulness of school and friends. When her parents divorced it was especially important as an anchor in her troubled world. That was the place where her confidence was sustained, her self-discipline was firm and some calmness had soothed the emotional nightmares of being at home. Within that memory of school as a shelter, there welled up inside Mary an enormous gratitude for the warmth and calmness of her schooldays. School had been the source of her energy, her commitment and her consistency. Somewhere in that experience, buried perhaps for ever, was the core of her vocation to teach and lead in school. It was a shock to find such energy and joy in an ordinary memory. It explained her desire to create order for young people, to radiate calmness and to show affection for youngsters under pressure.

In identifying that vague memory, Mary had touched her own personal vocation to teach and to lead. She had also recognised that need to create order and administer with the care of a king for the kingdom. She had come home to herself and to her life's work; the commitment that would give meaning to everything she would now do in her new role.

Case Study Two

Alan worked in a saw mill for five years before re-training and becoming a youth worker. Why he made the leap to youth work was a mystery, but he was desperately unhappy at the saw mill and had been for years. He enjoyed the change, the flexibility and the chance to be creative when faced with problems. He liked young people and found he could be friendly with them and yet he could challenge them. Now, faced with a challenge to move into a leadership role in the area youth office, Alan found he was uncertain. He had enjoyed face-to-face work with young people and felt it was his real strength. This new role was largely administration, supervision and policy development; it would take him out of face-to-face work for most of the week.

The money was really good though and it would make a difference to the mortgage. He turned the application form over and over in his hands. He could do the job, but he didn't feel comfortable about taking it on. He stuck the application in his pocket and went home for tea.

Over the tea-table, Alan pushed the application form across to his partner Debbie and asked her opinion. After a pause Debbie fixed him with a shrewd eye and asked why he was hesitating. Alan stumbled through an answer and in the end admitted that he didn't know why he felt uncomfortable. Debbie looked at him with real affection and told him he would be daft to take the job and then explained why he shouldn't. She reminded him that he left the saw mill because he was tired of administration, invoices, plans and policies. She recalled his first weeks as a youth worker when he came home excited, alive and happily exhausted with face-to-face contact with young people. Alan nodded and was relieved she saw it all so clearly. But there was more. Debbie told him he was a good youth worker because he cared about individual young people. She reminded him how close he had come to a criminal career until he got involved in a summer project on the estate. It was that project that changed his friendship group and gave him the confidence to move into a proper job. Alan realised that youth work had saved his life when he was only sixteen. He wanted to repeat that miracle in the lives of the kids on the estate where he now lived. That experience at sixteen was the source of his energy and satisfaction in his role in youth work. Debbie told him to tear the application up and stick it in the bin. *You've got a vocation to work with young people, don't lose it,* she said.

Leadership as Personal Vocation

These studies underline the importance of a spiritual dimension in the desire for leadership. There is always more than money involved. That other dimension is a spiritual awareness that links the needs of young people with the leader's own life story. Leadership is personal. It is only when a link is made between the needs of the young and the personal experience of the adult that the energy of a vocation can flow consciously into the task of leadership.

The demands of leadership are personal, depending not only on the gifts but also on the heartfelt commitment of the leader in maintaining a spirit within the community. For Mary, knowing why she was so keen to work with troubled pupils increases her motivation, sustaining her even when she is misunderstood and achieves no measurable result. Staying in a face-to-face role for Alan is something he is less likely to regret and his commitment to that one-to-one relationship will mature into a life-long commitment. For both of them the roads of their spiritual development and their professional development have come together. They combine professional skills with a spiritual wisdom. Each of them, in their own way, becomes a model and a leader. Mary and Alan point beyond themselves to deeper values and to the spirit that drives them forward to make a difference. They have found their vocation.

In a Christian setting the general spiritual dimension becomes more specific. The gospel offers images and stories that connect with that inner spirit. The same images help the community to share and celebrate what is deeply personal. In a Christian school or project it is possible to link the inner and outer dimensions of spirituality in symbols and stories that bind the community into a life-giving relationship that leads to growth and healing for all. For Mary the symbol of the Cross no longer represents simply a religious artefact that hangs around the school, it symbolises her struggle with every difficult child she meets in her new role. For Alan the misty picture of the good shepherd that used to hang in his family home is now more than nostalgia, it describes the kind of relationship he is living out with children on the street. The power of these Christian symbols to map the inner story allows the whole of a person's life to be transformed into patterns that release life and energy for others. The sacraments and stories of Christianity become sacred symbols that hold all life together. They can sustain, guide and open up life. They are the most precious gifts that we can hand on to future generations.

PRIEST (Mystic)	PROPHET (Idealist)	KING (organiser)
Aware of inner moods	Concerned about fairness	Sensitive to boundaries
Sensitive to patterns	Aware of motivation	Reconciling
Trusting intuition	Defending the vulnerable	Coordinating
	Impatient with fudges	Decisive
Concerned to heal hurts	Confronts hypocrisy	Interdependent
Searches for meaning	Challenges for change	Celebrates well
Needs time to reflect	Aware of the ideal	Guards dignity of all
Aware of symbolism		

Questions

Where are your strengths? Where are the gaps?

Which of the columns displays your strongest gifts?

Where have those gifts come from?

Which of the columns seems most urgent for you?

What memories come to mind to explain that energy?

How has the spiritual story of your life led to your role?

If these columns describe the Christian vocation, what do you need to work on?

Reflection

Thank you Lord for my vocation to leadership
In the service of the young.
The roots of this vocation tangle into the story of my life
Holding meaning and energy for my work
Holding me in a story of gospel love.

May I draw on the roots of my care for the young
Buried in my own history.
When energy is low and keeping going seems impossible
Help me sink my roots deeper into the motives and reasons
That touch my heart and history.
Then I can find the inner strength
For calmness, for consistency and caring
On behalf of the young.

The story of my work with the young
Has grown out of a shared story
In which I have been given much.
It is a story that has raised my awareness
That I have much to give in serving the young
So much to learn from working with them.

My calling has come through teachers I have known
Through family affirmation and from friendship.
My own desires for justice, order or nurture
Point to a need to make a difference
That will be hidden in young people for the future.
I need to touch these roots of my vocation often.
Recognising the wisdom that has led me to this life.
Unfolding in my memory is a story that will never end
Where the mysterious roots of my calling
Become the eternal embrace of God.

CHAPTER 3

SPIRITUAL LEADERSHIP & THE EASTER STORY

Every Christian community looks to the story of the Cross and Resurrection of Jesus, as a foundation stone of faith. The story opens up a mystery about who Jesus is, about how death is not the end, about the power of love and the significance of our suffering. Anyone who leads in a Christian school or project needs to make some connections between this core Christian experience and their daily practice of leadership in the community.

The story, often called *The Paschal Mystery* by Christians, involves a number of different elements:

The condemnation of Jesus to death

His crucifixion

Burial in a tomb

Resurrection

Ascension

Sending of the Spirit (Pentecost)

This sequence of events is a mystery that Christians live with every day, not just as a story from the past but as something that changes the way they think about themselves, their relationships and their actions in the present moment. The second Vatican Council expresses the reality of Jesus' paschal mystery in this way:

We who have been made like him, who have died with him and risen with him, are taken up into the mysteries of his life until we reign together with him.[6]

You will notice that the dying and rising in the quotation are in the past tense, even for us today. The Paschal Mystery is seen as a single event transforming all reality and revealing a pattern deep in all of creation that moves from death to life and to spiritual growth. It is something that is present now in all that happens and The Paschal Mystery pattern of events helps us to recognise how God might be working in a given setting such as a school or a project for young people.

---

6   *Lumen Gentium Pope Paul VI 1964*

This pattern in life, though already familiar, may not have been recognised. It is a pattern that is seen most clearly at times of crisis and change, those times when leadership needs to be most active. It is a pattern that operates in every culture and in each community. It is good news because it begins to make sense of the random patterns of life, giving them meaning and moving them towards a relationship of love and the mystery of God. An extended example might help to illustrate how this paschal mystery might unfold in a school setting.

Arthur has been deputy head for twelve years. He is a dedicated teacher and skilled in management. He is seen as solid and dependable in meetings and in timetabling across the curriculum. One morning however he forgot to prepare the cover lessons when there was a large number of staff away on courses. Chaos ensued. What was surprising was that Arthur didn't seem bothered. Weeks went by and other small signs appeared that things were not right. Books were overdue for checking, next year's timetable was not progressing and the number of short absences from his office coalesced into hours. The crunch came when the head teacher discovered two empty bottles of spirits in his office bin and two full ones in his filing cabinet while Arthur was absent. On returning to school the head teacher steeled himself and confronted Arthur and he readily admitted his drink problem, he even seemed relieved to talk about it.

The school was able to give Arthur time off, the leadership team gave support and encouragement and gradually Arthur returned to his usual efficient self. However, Arthur was never the same again. He had lost some of the hardness of the past and had found some compassion in dealing with other staff. His relationship to other members of the leadership group had warmed noticeably. He seemed more ready to ask for help and more grateful for any signs of affection. Somehow Arthur had changed.

This is a story that could happen in any school or project, at any time. It is also a story that mirrors the deeper reality of the paschal mystery. Arthur had experienced a marriage break-up and a precious relationship had died. He had been betrayed, he felt, by the one who meant most to him. The death of that relationship had left him entombed in depression, trapped in a deep loneliness and drinking was a way of managing that experience. He was relieved when it was discovered because it was the first sign of personal care he had received since his break-up. Unbelievably for him, many of his colleagues understood and showed the kind of affection that brought him back to life, into the land of the living. Even after that initial support faded, something, some spirit of optimism and trust, stayed with him. He was able to relate to others better; he appreciated others more and was more alive because of what had happened.

For Christians, stories such as this resonate with the deep pattern captured in the accounts of Jesus' death and resurrection. Sometimes the whole story is visible but often only fragments of this pattern are obvious. The young person, who after years of under-achieving and shyness, suddenly blossoms into a confident and lively person has experienced a kind of resurrection. Behind that *Resurrection Event* will have been some struggle, uncertainty and some of the trust that took Jesus through the Cross. The whole process of maturing for a teenager means dying to the childishness of earlier years in order to grow to fullness of life in adulthood. The story of promotion to leadership has a similar death-and-life motif, since increased responsibility means letting-go, dying to some of the behaviours and camaraderie of the past, in order to be a clearer role-model for the whole community.

Paschal Mystery and Leadership

The story of leadership will inevitably echo the pattern of *the paschal mystery*. Any leadership role that makes a difference and helps to transform the group or the community will have parallels in the dying and rising of Jesus. Some of these elements are listed below by way of illustration but each leader will live out this pattern in a unique and personal pattern of encounter with the risen Jesus.

Betrayal and Condemnation

Just as Jesus stood before Pilate and Herod and was condemned unfairly so the leader in a Christian community can expect to be let down and written off by many people in their time of leadership. It is part of human nature to look for a target for frustration and for blame. A leader is likely to attract such frustration and be the target of anger, sometimes for no obvious reason. Colleagues and young people are equally likely to identify the leader as the problem rather than the specific issue involved. The leader's attitude is attacked and becomes the focus of rumour and intrigue. The leader is misquoted and condemned in their absence by groups within the community.

The Paschal Mystery seems to suggest that such animosity be met by reason and calmness where possible. Jesus said little in his own defence and the leader may do well to imitate this economy of speech when faced with emotional outbursts from others. In doing so the leader takes their stand beside Jesus. The anger and confusion then take on a deeper and spiritual significance. The identification of the leader with the gospel story grows and they draw wisdom from the gospel tradition and a closer relationship to Jesus.

The Cross

There are so many ways that the Cross casts a shadow over leadership. Jesus experienced the Cross as a lonely place, where brutality ruled and he was a pawn in a game of politics between the Jews and the Romans. In a similar way a leader needs to cope with loneliness. At times the leader needs to stand alone with unpopular decisions and do what they believe is right. At times the leader will have to accept brutal judgements, put-downs and gratuitous anger from young people and colleagues alike. There is no place for the leader to hide from such negative and aggressive behaviour. The leader has, at times, to hold the ground on certain issues and for that they may well have to suffer. The leader can also be caught up in the politics of groups, issues and in the self-interest of individuals. They can be set up, overlooked and written off by team members and young people. In each of these situations Jesus held a clear focus on his Father and refused to change his mind or go back on what he had said. His words from the Cross continue to radiate compassion for others, for his family, for those crucified with him. Jesus' awareness of his Father on the Cross seems to grow stronger. That same focus on the Father is something that can sustain a Christian leader who is being targeted unfairly. Trusting that God as Father understands can strengthen the integrity and calmness of a leader under pressure. It allows the leader to recognise when it is worth arguing the case and when it is best to say nothing. It also underlines the importance of never giving up on showing compassion and kindness even when under pressure.

The Silence of the Tomb

Resurrection did not happen immediately in the paschal mystery. There were three days in the tomb. A time of emptiness, silence and waiting intervenes between cause and effect. New life does not spring directly from the Cross. In the task of leadership there are times of silence, waiting and uncertainty. There is the need to hold one's nerve as a leader when anger has overflowed, when painful things have been said and continue to trust in the goodness of those involved.

The Resurrection

The Resurrection came as a surprise. It was unexpected. Resurrection is a gift of God and not just the result of hard work or planning. Resurrection also happens quietly, in the dark of the night and it often upsets the status quo. Christian leadership is challenged to recognise the Resurrection in small changes in individuals and groups. For example, the absence of moaning from a group of young people may not seem much to the casual observer but to the astute leader it may indicate a deeper change to more life-giving relationships. The increased readiness of staff to volunteer for a fund-raising event might be a change that has no roots in the skills of leadership but is a deep response to the spirit in each person.

Resurrection is a gift that cannot be manipulated or even expected. It usually comes after some process of struggle but it depends on a personal response from individuals at a place where they are alone with their God. The role of the leader is not to control but to recognise these seeds of Resurrection and help them to grow through encouragement and support. The image of the seeds in a garden is appropriate here because the first appearance of the risen Jesus is in a garden; indeed Mary Magdalene mistakes Jesus for a gardener. The image of a gardener is one that a leader might usefully reflect upon in considering the tasks and style of spiritual leadership.

The Sending of the Spirit

Unlike the Resurrection, the descent of the Spirit on the disciples was not hidden or quiet. It took place in the light of day and among a group of people who were waiting and preparing for its arrival. The effects were not slow to develop. There was an immediate change in levels of confidence and enthusiasm. Energy and companionship increased. Courage, peace and joy broke out spontaneously as the pattern of past events fell into place. This collective experience was not a one-off euphoric moment. It fuelled a change in lifestyle that endured for the disciples' lifetime. It was the place at which the Christian Church was born.

The echoes of this Spirit still reverberate through the ethos of every Christian community. It is experienced individually and collectively at moments when a deeper pattern emerges in the daily routines of school and youth work. At an individual level this spirit may present itself as a certainty that one is in the right place and doing the right thing, a sense of harmony and a deeper logic that is accompanied by gratitude and joy. At a group level it may be experienced as a fluency in working together, mutual understanding, ease and unity filled with peace and the goodness of being together. This kind of shared experience is only achieved after other aspects of *The Paschal Mystery* are experienced, a point that will be explored in Chapter Four. The leader, recognising the spirit, needs to draw from it the energy and wisdom to renew their commitment. They need above all to remember the experience and return to it often in more difficult times ahead. As the Fathers of the Church used to say, *When in desolation remember consolation.*

Questions

Can you recall any moments of resurrection, surprising moments of new life and change in your work with young people or colleagues?

What would you describe as your greatest cross as a leader in a Christian community and what helps you shoulder that burden?

In what sense are you waiting for inspiration and energy in your work as a leader in a Christian community?

As you look back at your story of work with the young, what patterns of challenge and change seem to reflect the pattern of The Paschal Mystery?

Reflection

The rhythms of Cross and Resurrection
Ripple through history,
Through cultures that rise and fall
Through each season
The way of the Cross and Resurrection
Opens the pathway to meaning
To an eternal pattern
At the heart of creation.

The way we work with young people
Leads into patterns of change and challenge
With the growing pains of groups.
May these patterns lead us back into the mystery
Of Cross and Resurrection
Worked out in ordinary lives.
As a leader in a Christian community
May I be sensitive to the twists and turns
Of work with young people.

May I find strength in the presence of God
Not only in success but also in struggle.
Let me sense the mystery of a deeper life
In times of silence, and in suffering.
May I learn the wisdom of waiting
For the Easter pattern to unfold
In the lives of the young.

As I struggle with my own patience
With beginning again and again.
When I need to face new ways of working
With new policies and plans,
Help me trust to the deeper rhythms
Of life and love woven into life
In a Christian community.
May I root my deepest motives in mystery
Struggle, celebrate: wait and work,
In the hope of an eternal Easter,
Unfolding in the lives of all those
On the journey to resurrection.

CHAPTER 4
LEADERSHIP AS ANIMATION

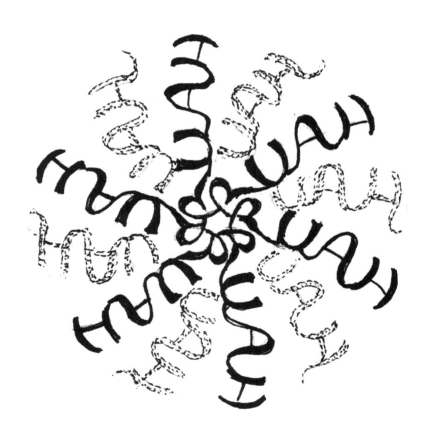

Leadership with young people often means becoming an educator or a trainer. These two modes of work with young people are essential. The first comes from the Latin word educare, to draw out, reminding educators that they are not pouring information into young people but drawing them towards their full potential in life. The second role of training involves the idea of forming and shaping young people for specific tasks for living and working in a complex world. Both these modes of working have a spiritual dimension since they involve respect for the unique pattern of gifts and the inner spirit of each young person. There is however a third mode of working with young people – animation. This approach has been part of the tradition of work with young people in Britain for over a century, joining good practice with the spiritual dimension of education in a more obvious and lively partnership.

Animation

Talk about animation usually conjures up visions of cartoon programmes such as *The Simpsons*. The term is appropriate to cartoonists because they animate or bring to life static pictures that can then tell a story. Animation comes from the Latin word *anima,* meaning soul. To animate therefore means to put soul into something, to recognise a deeper and perhaps spiritual reality within. Literally it means to breathe life into. The same phrase describes the way that God gave life to man and woman in the book of Genesis.[7] That breath of God, Ruah in Hebrew, is seen as the part of life we share with God, our spiritual life. So animation becomes an important model for leadership in a Christian community.

The tradition of animation is linked especially to the history of liberal education in Europe and emerged in Britain through youth movements such as the YMCA and the Boys Brigade, as well as broader social movements focused around specific settlements especially in London. Animation is the process of awakening and breathing life into individuals, groups and whole communities so that they can create for themselves and those around them a more life-giving environment. Notice that the focus is mainly on the creation of a stimulating environment rather than trying to stimulate individuals and perhaps robbing them of their inner freedom to choose. There is a focus on creating an atmosphere, an ethos, in which everyone can come to life and that life can overflow into the local community.

---

7   Genesis 2.7

This awakening and nurturing role depends upon an optimistic belief in a divine spark in each person. No one is written off. This is especially important in a highly secularised culture where measurement and money seem to be the only standards of value. As Hay and Nye observed in a study of spirituality in children:

The blotting out of spirituality is culturally mediated.[8]

The soul and the spiritual dimension of young people can be devalued by an over emphasis on individual success and measurable achievement. Animation also recognises the importance of participation, celebration, the joy of physical exercise, drama and art which tend to evade the cruder measures of a utilitarian ethos. Creating a community, developing participation, increasing democracy and building warm and supportive relationships are highly valued in the animation model of leadership. In these more intuitive activities, surrounded by clear boundaries and a nurturing emotional environment young people are animated, awoken in the spirit to a more holistic and healed sense of themselves. They have breathed deeply of a spiritual life.

The Animating Leader

The leader who wants to animate young people and the community needs to reflect on the spiritual as it is encountered in four dimensions of their work:

The Individual
The Community
Loving Kindness
Active Presence

The Individual

The animating leader believes and trusts in the basic goodness of each individual, however well that goodness may be disguised. It is a daily act of faith in the presence of God in people that is often sorely tested. In that attitude is an optimism about a person's ability to grow and change even the most embedded patterns of behaviour. The other concern of the animating leader is to protect the freedom of the individual to follow their own unique path within

---

8   David Hay & Rebecca Nye *The Spirit of the Child* (Jessica Kingsley Publishers 2006) p 57

the community. This is not an invitation to chaos but a readiness to put in place only the most basic structures of rules and to see that they are maintained. As young people mature, more and more freedom is offered to the point where they become the principal partners in their own education. Rules and discipline are always needed to guard against thoughtlessness and the darker influences of peer-pressure on individual freedom. Each person has a dignity and needs challenges and guidance through a quiet word in the ear or the influence of good friends within the community. This person-centred approach needs to work today with a curriculum and a pace of life that leave little space for the one-to-one approach. Indeed the one-to-one approach needs to be set in the context of good child-protection practice to preserve the right of the child at a vital level.

The Community

The animating leader has to be concerned with the whole environment within which young people live and work. The places where young people meet need to be bright, stimulating and well cared for. It is a sign of respect for others that the whole community work to keep schools and projects clean and tidy. The community should be a focus for a regular programme of events, challenges and celebrations that allow small groups to form around short-term projects. Within those groups learning happens that goes beyond the visible curriculum and touches the spiritual dimension of those involved. New roles are explored, personal gifts are discovered and tested, and self-image is clarified in the mirror of the group's response to individuals. The focus on the individual emerges within a community setting through the animator's ability to consult and offer choice, developing a democratic approach where possible. Some projects are developed that take groups beyond their own community to serve others, partly to develop their own gifts and partly to recognise the dignity of people in the neighbourhood. All of this work is achieved in an atmosphere of respect, understanding, affection and humour, creating an environment that is safe, nurturing and focused on the common good.

Loving Kindness

The place of balanced affection in animation is perhaps the central liberating element for young people. Above all else, this awakens the spiritual dimension in the lives of young people since it is the goodness from the leader that calls forth the goodness of the young person. The power of such a basic human attitude should come as no surprise to Christians who recognise God as love. One of the Church's pioneers of animation, a priest affectionately known as Don Bosco, said this about loving-kindness, *Young people need to know that they are loved.*

Such a simple comment lies at the heart of the animator's style of leadership. It was not enough for Don Bosco that young people were loved; they also had to know and feel that they were the focus of a balanced and generous affection. In other words, the leader has to establish a friendly and respectful relationship with those for whom they care. With that loving-kindness made obvious the animating leader can then guide, celebrate and reprimand without damaging the young person's freedom or dignity. This does not mean that the animator has to be soft on discipline; on the contrary, they must be clear and consistent. They must reprimand with reasoned kindness and not in the heat of anger. Only when a young person knows that they are loved can they really absorb the lessons of a reprimand even if they come to realise the wisdom of that lesson later.

Don Bosco regarded the quality of relationships as the key element in the holistic growth of young people. He likened loving-kindness to an electric current that connected adult and young person, energising and awakening the love of God in ordinary moments. Even in the nineteenth century, Don Bosco was also aware of the need for child protection policies to be in place; to ensure the safety of this relational style of work with young people. He recommended that no adult be alone with a young person and that the adults should intervene quickly when colleagues began to lose their temper with aggressive young people. Moreover, he recommended the development of leadership among older youths as a way of maintaining healthy peer groups and modelling good habits to younger members of the Christian community.

Active Presence

One aspect of animation that is particularly demanding and yet vital to its success is the active presence of the leader in the community and among the groups with whom they are working. It is in this availability to people that loving-kindness finds its clearest practical expression. The leader is prepared to *waste time* with colleagues, leave their door open and spend time getting to know a wide range of individuals. This approach means stepping beyond the narrow limits of roles and specific tasks to become a builder of community.

When a leader takes time to get to know people beyond the immediate work situation, to share concerns, identify interests and enthusiasms, the school or project is transformed into a community of persons. For schools this may mean being in the playground or the staff room on a regular basis. In youth projects it may mean closing up later than advertised or spending time on street work when the opportunity is right. Don Bosco used to say that a teacher who only appeared in the classroom remained simply that, a teacher. When that same teacher *wastes time*[9] with pupils in the playground they become a friendly presence because they have made a personal choice to be with young people. This is not friendship with young people, it is a friendly approach. All the normal professional safeguards still apply. The difference is that a free choice has been made to be present to young people.

The active presence also implies an attitude that allows interruptions. Being *present with* someone else may well cost finishing a piece of non-urgent work that will need to be completed later. It involves an open and welcoming attitude, being approachable and warm as an enduring disposition. In other words, the animator needs to be something of a saint!

Animation as a Vocational Choice

The path of animation is a spiritual choice for a leader in a Christian community. Its end point is what the Church calls holiness since it involves a form of unconditional love and self-sacrifice that takes the leader deeper into a spiritual relationship with the God of love. It is not an easy path but one that is rich in maturity and littered with hidden rewards in the form of deeper relationships and the lasting gratitude of the transformed lives of the young. The struggle to be present to young people shifts over time into a partnership with the mystery of God in the leader and in the young people. In a more mystical sense the animator becomes caught up into the love of God among people in and through the confusion of adolescent growth.

Animation is a way to God in ordinary life, a vocation hidden inside a profession. Not everyone can accept this. Many professionals may feel that they do not have the energy or the spirit to live this vocation. All that can be done is to try; and even to do it badly may well be better. There is energy and wisdom in the role that is available through relationship with colleagues and young people

---

9   See Mary McKeone *Wasting Time in School:*
    Secondary School Chaplaincy(1993 Daughters of St Paul)

once the path is undertaken. It does, however, take an act of faith in young people, if not in God, to begin.

An example of school-wide animation

Thornleigh College is a Salesian school in North West England working in the tradition of Don Bosco. After a long period of year-on-year expansion, the leadership group and the governors felt the need to strengthen the ethos and tradition of the school. A school-wide project was devised that would explore the ethos of the school through art and surveys of pupils, parents and past pupils. An artist was commissioned to guide the visual process and the school chaplain designed and conducted surveys of different parts of the school community. From the beginning, the intention was to involve the whole community in one single project and bring that to a celebration point highlighting the newly-expressed spirit of the school.

Data Collection

The project began with a school-wide survey, collecting information from staff and pupils about the following areas.

Best and worst aspects of school	Personal stories of the spirit of the school
Personal spiritual moments at school	Specific values rankings
Visual images of the school spirit	Emotional maps of the school site

These six areas provided over 10,000 pieces of personal data on the sensed spirit of the school. The collation of the data formed an early exhibition that opened up debate on predictable issues such as the state of toilets and the quality of discipline. What was more interesting was the number of stories that reported an immediate sense of belonging and warmth and an awareness of values being lived. The visual images were screened by the artists and pupils were invited to come back for further art workshops to develop their ideas. The results were presented at three exhibitions over the next six months and school-wide feedback and discussion continued around the visualisation of the school spirit. During this time the number of informal conversations about spirit and image gradually increased. The English department managed the stories, the maths department processed the data, the geography department mapped the emotions of the school and the art department offered daily support to the resident artist. The history department traced the spirit of the school back into the archives and the RE department worked with the chaplain on the spiritual tradition of the school. The whole school became engaged in a single extended conversation.

Drawing the process to a focus

Having widened the participation and involved parents, cleaners and canteen staff, the process needed to be drawn to a new focal point. The artist identified key themes and pictures and the local education authority artists were invited to help make a visual synthesis with pupils. The preferred image that emerged was a jigsaw piece.

A jigsaw is a simple shape that can carry the wide range of values emerging from the survey, yet also having some vital things to say about the spirit of community:

Each piece, like each person is unique
Each piece like each person needs to connect with others
A deeper picture emerging when we connect together

The school was badged with jigsaw pieces that carried the value-words, emerging from the survey. The artist spent some time creating a fine art piece and a large circular jigsaw of the spirit of the school and these were presented at a launch event which showcased the pupils and departments as they expressed the spirit of the school. The event was moving and a heartening celebration of deep spiritual values.

The project review that followed the launch realised that something like this process of opening up conversations and listening for the spirit should become a constant feature of school life. The following year, the focal point was on textile banners for the hall, how they would express the spirit of the school. The year after will be a jigsaw seating project creating an outdoor classroom and meeting space in partnership with the local university. There are no deadlines to these projects; they are focal points for conversations and examples of the whole community expressing its own spirit.

The Process

Throughout the process, the input of staff, pupils and parents was treated equally. Everyone was encouraged to participate. The quality of conversation improved and communication changed from being top down into a more complex pattern that carried not only information but personal feeling, motivations and values. In other words the process animated individuals and groups, clarified relationships and deepened motivation for sharing life together in a deeper spirit. Teachers worked with cleaners in art work sessions. Year 9 pupils interviewed parents and past-pupils about the spirit of the school, past and present. These conversations created opportunities to touch what was deepest in the relationships in a Christian community. The process opened an opportunity for quality listening in a variety of different ways. Because the focus was about feelings, experience and the spirit, it led to a recognition of a common and deep spiritual identity that emerged from the community and sustained the community. It was an animating process.

Outcomes

The school community is now more articulate about the spirit of the school. There is a wider and deeper sense of ownership of the ethos. Relationships have been strengthened between pupils and adults, between parents and teachers and between the present and past pupils. The school is visually enhanced with a whole school theme that is bright, expandable and flexible. The material developed is now being incorporated into school literature, on websites and publicity.

One specific outcome has been used as a shorthand explanation of the spirit of the school by drawing four of the more important values together from the school wide survey:

Respect
Understanding
Affection
Humour

These four values have been highlighted in stained glass in the school hall. They express the down to earth concern of pupils and staff about the way they want to relate. Yet, the initial letters RUAH also spell out the Hebrew word for breath and spirit. The use of the initial letters takes the behaviour dimension of the four values to the deeper level of motivation, to a spirit that animates and breathes *life* into ordinary life.

Questions

Where has your faith in the goodness of people, including yourself, been severely tested?

How much space do you give to consulting and listening in your style of leadership?

How do you express affection appropriately with young people and with colleagues?

How do you maintain a friendly presence with young people and colleagues that extends beyond the specific demands of the leadership role?

Do you find it easy to relax and celebrate alongside the young and with colleagues?

Have you made time for your own growth in understanding as a leader through reflection and through study?

Reflection

To put a smile on the face of a young person
Is to awaken the face of God in them.
To treat others with respect
Is to honour the mystery of the spirit
Moving them towards life.

In God we all live and breathe and have our being.
As educators we live that mystery each day
Breathing a life that will last for ever.
Inspiring the young with dreams of a better world
Healing unknown hurts with hope
Mending broken hearts and dreams
With practical help and consistent care.

The spirit moves us when we get angry
Because others' rights are not respected.
The same spirit sheds light into our minds
When answers appear as if from nowhere.
When compassion for colleagues or young people
Makes a home in our heart
It is the same spirit bridging their needs
and our care for them.

The spirit is at work in us when joy bubbles up unbidden.
There is joy in achievements, in endings and beginnings
In accidents and in awareness that all is well
The spirit of celebration slips into the spaces of each day.

May we, as spiritual leaders, be aware of that spirit
When it arises in colleagues and young people.
May we pause long enough to greet the spirit
With respect, understanding, affection and humour.
As it slips through the spaces between people
May the spirit bring to life that which will last for ever.

CHAPTER 5
TEAMWORK & AUTHORITY

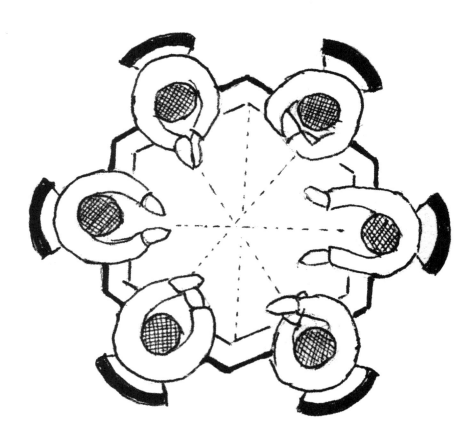

Don Bosco, a great Christian educator, was accused by some Christians of not building enough penance into his style of working. He replied that if one really lived and worked lovingly with other people in community there would be enough penance without going to look for it. Good teamwork and the exercise of authority draws the Christian leadership into hope and human frailty where disappointment and frustration will also be the spur to greater maturity and spiritual growth in the leader.

The spirit of Christian teamwork and authority is quite different from many of the business models that abound in western culture. Even after two thousand years, the words of Jesus speak eloquently and with a deep challenge to the secular and spiritual leaders of today:

> **You realise that in business and politics leaders like to make their authority felt and to use leadership for their personal advantage. That must never happen with you. If you want to be a leader you must regard yourself as a servant, and anyone who wants to be first must become last of all. You must follow the example of the Son of Man who came not to be served by other people but to serve and give his life away for others.**[10]

This is a foundational scripture text for all in authority. It demands a deeper level of motivation and sacrifice in leaders of a Christian community. Modelling service and self-sacrifice is intimately bound up with the authority. Within that Christian context, leaders will often be challenged to turn the other cheek, to be a Good Samaritan and to go the extra mile with colleagues and young people in order to achieve the spiritual aims of their role as leader. These roles may not be in any job description but they are all implied in the need to model a Christian ethos and form a Christian community with young people.

Alongside authority lies a more personal style of leading a team, be it a leadership team or a department in a school or a youth club team or catechetical group in a parish. Teamwork demands a personal approach and a level of self knowledge that is not afraid to open up strengths and weaknesses in a team. No team is perfect. It still needs to achieve its goals, sustain a healthy pattern of relationships and care for individual needs. In Christian terms, the team is a small community where life is shared, gifts explored, hurts are healed and each person grows in wisdom, on their own faith journey. The spiritual leader

---

10   Matthew 20.24-28 paraphrased

is asked to attend to this deeper dimension and to raise awareness of the spirit in the ordinary events of life in teams and decision-making.

Teamwork

Teams are an amalgam of gifts, motivations, blind spots, personal histories and emotions that need to be blended and focused on a specific task if the team is to work well. The chemistry of the team mixture can be volatile or lifeless at times. The task may be clear or vague. The nature of the team's role may demand a highly democratic approach or a very decisive style of leadership. In each case the personal style of the leader will be crucial.

The leaders need to be aware of their personal preferred style of leading and perhaps expand the repertoire of styles as they become established in the role. In leading his own disciples, Jesus speaks about his friendly style with the ones he worked with:

> **I call you friends because I have shared with you everything I have learnt from the Father.**[11]

This aspect of leadership links in with the centrality of loving-kindness in animating others. Engaging other team members in a friendly way and generating a friendly atmosphere opens up confidence, liberates gifts in the team and helps to heal disputes and support individuals. A friendly approach sets the spirit free. This friendly approach can make teams effective even if the leader lacks large areas of competence. The leader does not need to be perfect or an expert in order to pull the team together. Consider this example of Christian leadership in a parish setting.

Case study: Phil, a leader who thrived on failure

Phil has been a leader for many years and has managed a number of projects in parishes and inner city youth settings. He has been highly successful and accomplished a huge amount of good for young people and trained a large number of youth workers, some of whom are in senior posts in youth services. From this brief description you may well conclude that Phil is highly skilled and competent. Perhaps he is, but not in the way you might expect.

---

11   John 15:15

Phil is disorganised, poor in taking minutes, finds it difficult to evaluate events and to manage his time effectively. This might seem to be a recipe for disaster except for one fact: Phil is aware of his weaknesses. With those in mind he builds a team that can complement his other gifts. Phil is inspiring, excellent with young people and able to celebrate individuals and affirm their gifts. In building a team Phil is also very humble, admitting his weakness and asking for the kind of support he needs in his role. There is nothing of the heavy hand of authority in this style but genuineness and a deep commitment to serving the young that is visible and inspiring to others.

Phil's leadership style is based on his ability to panic. A common pattern in team meetings is for Phil to outline the needs of young people and express the outline of a plan to meet the need. As the amount of work to achieve the plan became clear Phil would panic about how to do it all, where to get resources, how to communicate and deal with health-and-safety issues. As the issues were raised, different team members would ease Phil's panic by taking responsibility for different areas. It was obvious to the team members that Phil could not do these tasks and they were happy to fill that gap. What emerged was an effective plan, based on good teamwork that reflected the skill gaps of the leader. This only worked because the goodness and energy of Phil disarmed and engaged the gifts of others. Phil's skill was in his expression of his love for young people and his honest acceptance of his own weakness. The gap between his desire and his skill in working for the young became the space in which a team blossomed.

Phil's experience underlines the importance of being genuine and open in Christian leadership. Humility about one's own weakness and appreciation of others' gifts can create a sense of community that eases many of the frustrations of team work. Phil stands as an encouragement to being honest about strengths and weaknesses and finding the truth that sets people free in teams. Christian leadership integrates failure as part of *The Paschal Mystery* at work in the group. Some teams use specific personality surveys such as the *Myers Briggs Personality Inventory* or the more readily available *Keirsey Temperament Sorter* to explore gifts and weaknesses. Some teams seem to be able to reach an effective level of honesty through conversation and kindness.

A friendly style of leading teams

Teamwork books can be found in abundance and they explore the tasks, processes and skills of teams at different stages of their development. For

Christian leadership all those views can be useful as long as a friendly style of animating the group is at work. The importance of compassion, failure, forgiveness and affection connects the spiritual leader to their team in a unique spiritual relationship. This personal and friendly approach lifts leadership to a new level and gives it access to motivation and to a vision that can engage a spiritual energy for the team.

The leader is not necessarily a friend to each member of the team but their approach to team members needs to be friendly. In exploring how this friendly style might look for different people a Christian leader might consider the following listing from a recent study on friendship by Tom Rath.[12] Each person will identify with a number of these overlapping styles of friendship and others will feel unnatural. Those that do engage with the reader might lead to a reflection on a personal and friendly style of leadership and the skill gaps that might need to be filled by other team members in a friendly approach to leadership.

Builders	Increase motivation in others, are ready to advise on how to build strengths and overcome weakness. They are generous in spending time with others.
Champions	Will defend others when under attack and will be fiercely loyal to the integrity of others. They will give praise often and in public about others.
Collaborators	Enjoy sharing decisions and activities and are sensitive to the need to involve others and gain their approval, if not permission, for activities.
Connectors	Spend time getting to know a person and able to link people through common interests and backgrounds to create a life-giving network in the team.
Energisers	Able to have fun, celebrate and bring some joy and optimism into relationships when times are hard. They tend to be earthy characters.
Mind Openers	Keen to explore new ideas and open up a bigger vision that gives a context and meaning for day-to-day activity.

---

12   Tom Rath *Vital Friends* (Gallup Press 2006) (Only the 8 titles are taken directly from the book)

Navigators	Skilled in guiding at a personal level when the normal patterns of energy and action seem to break down.
Companions	Present, available and ready to waste time with people. Companion is a Christian-rooted word that describes someone who shares bread.

Christian leaders, considering these eight friendship styles, might find much to affirm their personal style of working with individuals and teams. They may also find some aspects of friendship and leadership in which they are weaker. Admitting these weaknesses, at least to oneself, is a vital part of maintaining a genuine and humble approach to leadership. The same listing could be used by a leader to reflect on team-members, their own gifts and skill-gaps so that the friendship base of the team can be maintained and deepened through time. Keeping a focus on both strengths and weaknesses awakens the compassion, forgiveness, realism, recognition of growth and celebration that the gospel inspires. With that focus on frailty and humility in teamwork many of the training manuals on teamwork reach a greater depth and the challenge of team work becomes a faith journey for the group and each individual.

Authority

Authority is the part of leadership that gives a freedom to act, to make decisions and to expect others to comply. Jesus' words about how this authority should be used have already been quoted. The source of authority for Jesus came from his relationship with God as a Father which led him to recognise the dignity and freedom of each person. For that reason he was able to challenge the hypocrisy he encountered in religion and speak with authority to the darker and damaged parts of people's lives. He was able to guide his team of disciples, set standards and reprimand them when the time was right.

All of this authority was something Jesus possessed as a natural style and yet it was also given to him from his Father. This double source of authority is something that most leaders are familiar with. A departmental head has been given authority to organise a subject area and deliver the curriculum across a school. Authority is delegated *from above*. There is also another type of authority that is more personal and subtle that needs to emerge in the particular network of relationships within which the leader works. This informal authority grows through the leader's own commitment, genuine care for those involved and an adequate level of competence in their role. This type of authority rather than being given from above is offered to the leader from the team and the young people with whom the leader is working. One wise person observed that, in any classroom in the country, teachers only have the power to lead and teach because the class gives them that authority. It is the same with teams; the leader only leads in the long run with the consent of the team. The team that is listened to, consulted, celebrated and guided is far more likely to give authority to the leader than the team that is spoken down to, ignored and criticised angrily.

In exercising authority, a leader has to live with the tension between the needs of delivering the task and the needs of the individuals involved in the task. At times the task will come first and at other times the needs of relationships and individuals will need to prevail. From the outside the leader looks powerful, able to make decisions and carry authority. From the inside, the leader may often feel torn between meeting one priority and disappointing a number of people who would want other priorities to be met. The experience for the leader is not one of being powerful but rather of being helpless in meeting all the needs in the group. The leader is stretched between limited resources and unlimited needs. Like Jesus, stretched on the Cross, they are often surrounded by misunderstanding and verbal abuse. Their authority is, at times, a source of suffering rather than an experience of power.

Authority and Ruah

The four elements of *Ruah* suggest practical ways to exercise power in a balanced way that reduces the possibility of damage in the exercise of authority.

1. **Respect** suggests that the leader needs to listen carefully and consult widely before making a major decision. The need to take the team along with decisions and allow problems to be raised is essential to gain acquiescence, if not approval, for the decision. The way that decisions are communicated is also a part of respecting individuals, especially when decisions are unwelcome. Bad news should be shared and explained face-to-face with team members and not communicated remotely by mail or notice boards.

2. **Understanding** suggests that a leader needs to realise, as far as possible, the full implications of a decision before its implementation. This applies not only to the particular way of working together but also for the individual change and challenge it might imply for team members. Here, a quiet word in the ear and an ability to absorb some frustration or perhaps to ease the way a decision is implemented can help to demonstrate that the leader understands the whole picture and does care.

3. **Affection** is a quality that has to be laid down in advance in the team if they are to manage hard decisions. The leader, through affection for each team member builds a bridge of confidence with them. Hard decisions can test the strength of that confidence and, sometimes, the team-member will withdraw affection. The Christian leader, inspired by the gospel does not break the bruised reed or quench the faltering light of the candle but continues to extend affection, even when it is not returned. This situation places the leader in the position of the loving father waiting for the prodigal son to return home (see Luke 15.11-24). It is another experience of powerlessness for the leader in the exercise of their rightful authority.

4. **Humour** is an essential gift for dealing with the exercise of authority. The ability to put the mechanics of roles aside, to relax and play, produces a wider perspective and allows authority to fit into a wider pattern of group roles. The ability of leaders to laugh at themselves, to escape intensity and seriousness on occasion, allows them to grow in authority.

Dealing with Confrontation in Christian Leadership and Teams

When people with different abilities, expectations and stories meet to work together, differences may emerge that can lead to conflict.

This is a normal situation for Christian leaders to face and the absence of conflict for long periods should ring alarm bells for the leader. Conflict is part of the growth-process of the group, when managed effectively it can lead to a deeper awareness and maturity. It is part of the Cross that can lead to Resurrection and a deeper spirit of cohesion in the team.

Recognising conflict in its early stages can help with its management. The silence of a team member at a meeting might provoke a phone call by the leader to check if all is well. The insistence on a small and specific detail in a plan may conceal a hidden antagonism that needs addressing. Whenever the negative emotional force invested in comments seems to outweigh the importance of the issue there will almost certainly be some conflict in the background. It may be conflict at home, grief issues or health and little to do with the team itself. However, unless it is recognised and confronted, the issue will inevitably disturb the team.

Confronting conflict is never easy. Even the most experienced of leaders find it difficult. To confront means to bring an issue into face-to-face recognition. It is important to do this in a Christian community because the truth that will set us all free is shared among individuals. It is only when the leader can see what others see that the conflict can be seen positively and managed effectively. Confrontation is not telling someone off but rather a process of listening and speaking so that a bigger picture emerges about the behaviour of the team.

The first question a Christian leader needs to ask is, *Why do I want to confront?* If I am motivated by real concern for the other person and a sense of responsibility for the team, then confrontation will probably succeed. If the leader is motivated by a desire to put someone in their place, settle an old score or express a general frustration with progress, then confrontation will be doomed from the start. If a leader is angry with a team member, they should avoid confronting them in that mood. It could be that another team member may be better placed to hear the situation from the other person. The key point is to look at the bigger picture, to understand the other's situation and maintain a positive relationship as far as possible.

To be effective in confronting another person a Christian leader needs to keep respect for the individual at the forefront of their thoughts. The person they are dealing with is a son or daughter of God, however awkward or complicated they may seem. Agree a time when there is enough space in the programme to talk and listen. Prepare what you will say in the form of observable behaviour and not hearsay. The behaviour needs to be confronted in the present and nothing else. It is tempting to bring up old history or to suggest motivations for behaviour. Neither of these is helpful in confrontation. Above all, the leader needs to be direct, specific and gentle in manner. Having spoken clearly, be prepared to stop and wait and listen to the response. For some people, that might involve coming back at another time when they have absorbed what has been said.

Confrontation is an act of faith for the leader in a Christian community. It implies that the struggle to understand and manage conflict is a worthwhile activity. Living the tension between people in groups is a growing pain for all teams. For the Christian leader, that tension is given deeper meaning by the gospel and *The Paschal Mystery* in particular. Persevering in the struggle to work with others, whether in teams or in families, means that our efforts are stored like treasure in heaven, part of an eternal pattern that cannot be lost. Therefore faith and leadership walk hand in hand in a Christian community and leaders find ever deeper reasons for self-sacrifice and love for others.

Questions

Which, if any, of the eight styles listed in the table describe your approach to leadership most accurately?

What are your strengths and weaknesses in managing conflict?

How do you cope with failure?

In what ways do you feel you inspire, reward and guide those you lead?

How is leadership as *humble service* expressed in your present way of working?

Reflection

(An act of personal commitment to leadership)

Lord, help me to shoulder the yoke of leadership,
With a gentle and yet determined heart.
Make me humble and honest in living the truth,
Be understanding of team limitations.

May I respect the weakness of others
And not hide my own.
Help me to recognise your presence in failure
As well as in success.

In working together,
Let your spirit inspire each team member
And may I be sensitive to the spirit,
Moving in every emotion.

Help me to nurture the gifts of the team,
By encouraging each effort.
May I notice the silent triumphs of individuals,
With a quiet word of recognition.

Let me find time to waste with the people I lead,
To appreciate their strengths and struggles,
To laugh and be quiet with them.

Help me to notice and nurture the positive support,
Shared between members of the team.
May I be a shepherd of your loving kindness,
In all that I do.

Teach me Lord to model your kindness
and honesty in leadership,
To confront in the right way and at the right time.
To praise regularly, to reassure and guide with wisdom.
May I find the time to celebrate whatever happens,
Being a reminder to everyone
Of your loving presence living in people.

CHAPTER 6
DECISION-MAKING & SPIRITUALITY

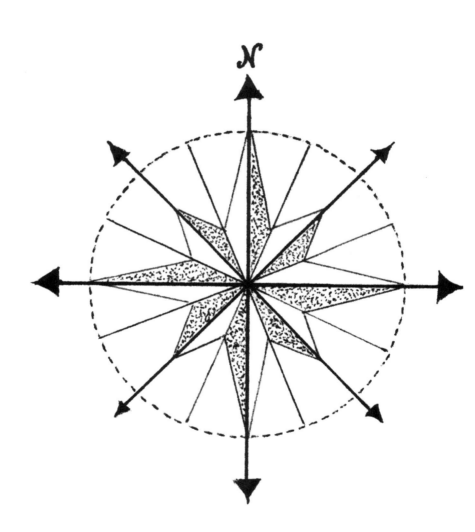

Schools and youth services, encouraged by OFSTED (Office for Standards in Education), have developed powerful tools for target setting. These targets need to be specific and measurable if accountability is to be achieved and funding guaranteed for the future. Spirituality and religious development do not always lend themselves to such specific and measurable outcomes. As a result they can sometimes be seen as marginal, privatised and optional elements in the decision-making process of a school or youth group. When everything has been measured, targeted and costed, there is always something more to be recognised and appreciated in what has been decided. Professional educators realise that even detailed plans and targets are only thumbnail sketches of a reality that runs into moods and meanings that will never be completely caught in the logic and language of organisation.

The fact that something cannot be measured does not make it of less value: pain and love cannot be measured and yet they are real experiences that have real effects on behaviour. In a similar way perhaps, the religious and spiritual dimension can have profound effects on individuals and groups. Social cohesion, self esteem, identity, courage, altruism and mental health all improve with religious practice but not in an easily measurable way over short timescales. The spirit moves at a deeper level than observable outcomes but it still needs a place in every level of decision-making, from weekly programmes to long-term development plans.

Organising from a spiritual perspective

In Genesis 12.1 God calls Abraham *to leave this land for the place that I will show you.* Abraham was not presented with a complete plan but an invitation. Neither was he given a precise destination point. Abraham had to leave the security of his own home before more details were offered. In other words, Abraham was not following a plan but entering into a relationship with God which had uncertainty and trust at its heart. There is a risk element here that involves setting out without specific outcomes. A parable might help to illustrate this element of uncertainty:

A man wanted to plant a tree. He dug a hole, found a healthy sapling, prepared the ground and planted the tree. To protect the young tree from storms he tied it to a wooden stake and waited. The tree died, the stake grew into a tree!

The unintended outcome of the plan points to the need for an openness to the unforeseen and a need for adaptability as things change. The story also suggests that, despite all our self-conscious cleverness, we are not always aware of the depth and complexity of the reality we might face. In the Second Vatican Council, the Church was described as *pilgrim people* journeying through time. The organisation needed for that journey is exploratory. New directions need to be investigated, mistakes made and a way forward decided upon. Even the mistakes are part of the process since the aim of the Christian journey is to travel deeper into relationship with the mystery of God. Failure can achieve that aim as well as success in making choices about the future. Therefore planning and evaluating in the Christian community has a faith dimension that needs another mindset and different tools for evaluation to complement the more structured forms of planning in use at present.

Map, Compass and Process in Spiritual Organisation

On a journey into a new landscape a map and compass are very useful tools that help to identify both location and direction. A map is only useful when some features on the map connect with the place in which one is standing. A compass is only useful if it is safe from deviation and trusted by its user. The Christian tradition offers the gospel as a map of experience and an inner spirit that calls each person back to the Father. A process is needed that draws the other two aspects into a way of thinking that links reality, spirit and the gospel into harmony. The pastoral cycle described below is the third element of guidance for good leadership in a Christian community.

The Gospel

The gospel is not a just a story about what has already happened. It is also a description of what still happens in all human life, culture and creation. The gospel patterns opened up in the life of Jesus reveal a pattern that is at work in every school and youth group. In order to read this pattern, it is important to recognise where the everyday events of life are reflected in the gospel. Having recognised the pattern, the gospel story then opens up an older and deeper mapping of what might be happening in those everyday events.

Case Study: Life-experience, Gospel and Planning

There have been problems in Year 10 among the girls. It has been clear that individual pupils have been isolated and ignored by their peers for weeks at a time. Colleagues have mentioned the issue and yet none of the girls has made a formal request for help. One of the staff mentions that these individuals seem to have become lepers in their year. The word *leper* reminds the Year Head about a story from the gospel and they look it up in chapter five of Luke. Reflecting on the story, it is clear that Jesus waited until he was approached by a leper before any change could happen. Jesus enquires if the leper really wants to be cured. The leper is then touched, and reconnected to the community through a formal priestly recognition of belonging.

The Year Head, reflecting on the story decides to adopt a policy of waiting until the girls make a formal complaint and not to interfere too quickly. When a complaint is made the policy would be one of connecting quickly and positively in a therapeutic way at a personal level. Finally, the pupil would be drawn into an affirming, shared event where a renewed sense of belonging could be celebrated.

This is a very limited example of how life and gospel might work together to support reflection and planning. The same gospel patterns will work in departments, in group experiences, and at whole school level. Some parts of the gospel lend themselves to this kind of thinking more than others. Stories that involve transformation, miracle stories and parables have a lot to say about change and how to manage it. Teaching sections of the gospel such as the Beatitudes offer some basic values for living together in community. Above all the story of the Cross, Resurrection and Pentecost offer a mapping of experience that gives meaning and significance to the whole of life. They are examples that might encourage the reader to establish clearer connections between the gospel and their own life experience.

The Spirit

The Book of Genesis describes human beings as sharing the breath of God's life. They have God's spirit within them. The experience of spirit is the part of us that is aroused by mystery, angered by injustice, hungry for relationship and crying out for meaning. The spirit acts as an inner compass, operating through inspiration, intuition and imagination, offering a different type of knowledge and a deeper level of motivation for living. This is the spirit that binds society together, energises moral choices and leads to an awareness of mystery and meaning in ordinary experience.

The spirit is an inner compass that draws us back to the unspoken source of all life. It is the intuition that preceded all moral decisions, acts of love, compassion and self-sacrifice. It is the experience of being overwhelmed by beauty, mystery and wonder. The spirit leads to an awareness that only limps into language, but it is an awareness that makes us human. In secularised thinking such immeasurable elements are relegated to a subjective and private world that is beyond the concern of measurable outcomes. When an organisation only plans with what can be measured by numbers then the spirit has been ignored and the compass for the journey has been lost.

A Christian community needs to create space in a deliberate way for the spirit to work. Pauses in the planning process, perceptive consultation with the wider community, the use of imagination, sensing the energy around various proposals and taking decisions into more formal moments of reflection can all put the spiritual compass back into the hands of leadership. This is not a sophisticated process; it is our natural way of working in community that has been deflected by a society that is focused on just one type of measurable knowledge.

The knowledge that we need for community planning will be specific and measurable if it is to be effective but first of all it needs to be rooted in spiritual knowledge. The knowledge needed is already hidden in the awareness of the people who make up the community and it is especially clear when they stand in a specific religious tradition. Consultation in planning is a gathering of the spirit, scattered through the community, a raising of shared awareness and an intuitive sensing of the energy for change and development. Building on spiritual knowledge and moving towards more specific planning ensures that plans are rooted in a communal motivation and not placed like a veneer over an uncommitted community.

The Pastoral Cycle

Schools and youth projects have some complex and difficult decisions to make on a regular basis. How does a school choose between upgrading toilets and employing another special needs teacher? What does a youth project do when funding suddenly has strings attached that do not match its core values? These value-based issues trigger ethical and spiritual questions that need careful reflection from leadership. Every budget option is a value issue and spiritual thinking should be as evident in the balance sheet as it is in the mission statement of a Christian community. The mission statement and policies of a

Christian community may not offer much guidance when hard decisions are called for. So how does a leader make good spiritually-balanced decisions in large-scale planning?

Another type of decision arises not from the predictable planning decisions of a year but from the unpredictable accidents and opportunities that land on a leader's desk sometimes on a daily basis. These surprises vary from the disaster about to happen to a window of opportunity to do something that was not in the plan. To what extent does a leader adapt to events, how do the gospel and the spirit speak to day-to-day emergency decisions?

A third type of decision-making focuses on the needs of the young people and the team being led. There will be a wide spectrum of needs within the leaders remit: the need for challenge, encouragement, guidance, discipline and training. How do Christian leaders view their task of guidance of the people in their care? How do leaders decide how to manage the mesh of relationships in which they are called to work?

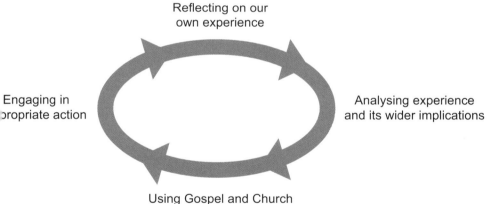

Reflecting on our
own experience

Engaging in
propriate action

Analysing experience
and its wider implications

Using Gospel and Church
tradition to develop reflection

This circular pattern is a kind of spiritual map-reading. It involves reading the situation, knowing what is going on in terms of facts and feelings. The focus of the reflection is usually an opportunity for change. The feelings are important because they represent the energy for change and perhaps an expression of the spirit in action. There then needs to be some analysis so that what has happened can be seen in a bigger setting. Is everyone experiencing the same thing or is it just us? What patterns of cause and effect might be at work, what is good and what is damaging about the situation?

Having remembered experience, analysed the situation as a group, the process then leads to the gospel and tradition of the Church. Has anything like this happened before? Are any parts of scripture triggered by the reflection so far? This stage of the process needs some knowledge of the gospel but also a sense of imagination and intuition that can make the connections between gospel and the situation reflected upon. For Christians, reflecting on the gospel with a specific situation in mind, it is the Spirit that inspires and guides the links between scripture and reality.

Having identified some gospel pattern or values in the situation, the group is then challenged to let those ideas inform a plan of action. This leads to practical planning for change and development in the way things happen. Finally the whole process returns to reflection after the group has lived the changes they have planned.

This integration of reality, spirit and gospel is a form of discernment that leads to better decisions, a stronger sense of community and a wiser leader. The process may take ten minutes in a very specific or urgent setting or ten months if it involves long-term planning. The pastoral cycle illustrates a way of thinking that could become a way of life for the leader in a Christian community. It is the way that the leader can guide within the tradition and draw strength from it. It is part of the vocation to leadership in the Church.

Listening

One of the key elements in the pastoral cycle is listening. It is worth highlighting this skill for leadership because it can energise the reflection process when it happens. In the normal pattern of a day we hear a lot of words but their significance escapes us. The leader who listens establishes good relationships, encourages further honesty and knows more clearly what is happening. Most adults in the leader's team will need a good listening-to much more than a good talking-to. Anxiety and anger can be earthed when a colleague is listened to carefully by their leader. Listening can deepen companionship and release a team's energy to serve the young.

To listen takes courage on the leader's part. At times, the team may want to blame the leader for what is happening, or even undermine the leader's role in the team. Courageous listening takes leaders into a lonely role within the group where they may have to hold information and tensions without sharing those with others in the team. Listening for what is not said, listening for patterns of conversation and behaviour allows the leader to identify needs in the team. The needs may have to be dealt with openly as a recurring issue or quietly with a word in the ear. The moods of the team might provoke the leader to organise a celebration event, some training or even time off.

Listening for the needs of young people is a vital part of the reflection process if the work is to be life-giving. In a school or youth project the leadership needs to review what needs are being presented and if they can be met appropriately by the school or project. Young people have many needs that are impossible to meet in just one context. Most family needs cannot be addressed by a school and the formal educational needs of young people cannot usually be met in a youth project. The Search Institute[13] has created a listing of the basic needs of young people which is designed to be used by a whole community to review the needs of young people. The needs are broken down into external and internal assets needed for the healthy growth of young people. The external needs include basics such as positive adult relationships, boundaries and expectations, time at home, and positive peer influence. Internal assets include commitment to learning, caring, restraint, self-esteem, and sense of purpose and a positive vision of the future. The whole list of forty assets can be viewed on the website. The listing of basic needs required for youth to flourish has been researched extensively. It is another way for an individual leader or a whole school to listen with care to the needs of the young people they serve.

A Church-based Structure for Evaluation

A helpful structure to support reflection on work with the young has been provided by the Catholic Bishops of the USA. The outline below could be used as an evaluation tool in formal as well as informal settings in a Christian community. The bishops offer three goals in working with youth:

> To empower young people to live as disciples of Jesus Christ in our world today.
> To draw young people into responsible participation in the life, mission and work of the Catholic community.
> To foster the total personal and spiritual growth of each young person.

As a leader in a Christian community and working with young people these goals imply an ability to connect young people to the life of the Church community as

---

13   www.search-institute.org/assets

part of the ethos and context of the work. The goals assume some knowledge of gospel and Church and an ability to talk positively about it with young people. These three goals of discipleship, participation and personal growth need to find a home in wider planning structures and raise specific questions about the authenticity of the service offered to the young.

In a more specific way the Bishops have suggested that there are at least eight components of service to the young that need to be addressed if the above goals are to be met:

Advocacy	Defending, protecting and speaking for young people at risk within the community.
Catechesis	Learning to use scripture, prayer and experiencing Christian life as expressions of a personal relationship with Jesus.
Community	Having a sense of belonging and an identity that extends into a wider Church sharing of life and love.
Evangelisation	To awaken a call to follow the gospel and make a difference to our world especially by the example of adult discipleship.
Justice and Service	To recognise the needs of the poor and oppressed and to start with love and self-sacrifice.
Leadership Development	To identify and encourage the gifts of leadership among the young through practical roles and training.
Pastoral Care	A community-based response to the needs of the young modelled as a form of gospel love.
Prayer and Worship	Celebrations of faith with preparation and participation, including silence

This listing provides an outline of some of the ways that Church-based schools and projects envisage their role as it goes beyond that of a secular organisation doing similar work. It may be helpful in identifying the specific Christian dimension of the leader's task within the community. The listing may serve as a way of reviewing the way young people are served in a uniquely Christian style.

Questions

How would you assess your own organisation against the eight components of service to young people listed above? Where are the foundations for growth?

Can you remember a time when you were able to listen carefully and sensitively to an individual? What spiritual questions did that experience raise for you?

How would you go about listening spiritually to large groups of young people and teams of colleagues?

Where have you seen a gospel pattern unfolding in your work with others?

Reflection

Consensus and listening costs time.
Slowing decisions down to reflect
Becomes an act of faith that only a few may understand.

Leadership lives in a lonely place
Where it must stand alone before God,
And choose the best way to plan
For the spirit to grow stronger in its own setting.

Shepherding the spirit takes the leader
Through and beyond measured targets and outcomes,
Into a relationship of trust with God.

Planning for the spirit takes the leader
Into a dance with the divine,
Hidden in each member of the community.

Planning and teamwork guides a leader
Into a treasure-trove of giftedness in people,
Just waiting to be opened up.

Evaluation and assessment, done well,
Reveal and recognise the need
For healing and change in community.

As times change and confusion threatens,
It is tempting to think that everything is different.
But the old pathways of the gospel
Are still to be found in the humanity of colleagues,
In the hearts of the young.
Those paths may be ignored and overgrown,
But they still lead to life and the energy for change.
The gospel paths still run through the centre of each heart,
To promise a unity that is beyond imagination.

Such paths need to be found through listening,
Through planning and in gospel reflection each day.
For it is on those paths that the leader
Will walk with Jesus and find new energy,
To build teams and plan for a new future.

CHAPTER 7
SPIRITUAL LEADERSHIP & CURRICULUM

The curriculum in both youth work and formal education have focused largely on the acquisition of skills and measured outcomes in learning. Much spiritual awareness does not lend itself to such skill-based measurement especially over the relatively short periods involved in evaluating learning with young people. Spirituality is not, first of all, a skill or something that we acquire, there is a sense in which spirituality acquires and envelops each person, taking them beyond what is measurable towards what resonates beyond and within each person, with mystery and enticing truth and beauty. This kind of language does not sit easily within the framework of curriculum, assessment and evaluation and yet both the OFSTED (Office for Standards in Education)[14] and The National Occupational Standards for Youth Work[15] give prominence to the spiritual in attempting to evaluate work with young people.

These documents speak of the importance of wonder, compassion, acceptance, mystery, integrity, spiritual values, service, commitment, celebration, meditation, curiosity and many other aspects of spiritual life. Such values rarely appear in the official evaluations of schools and projects or in communications to parents and service users. The gap between the spiritual aspirations of Government documentation, and day-to-day evaluation structures, leaves leaders with the impression that the spiritual has been recognised and yet sidelined. The truth is that managers tend to focus on what can be seen and measured and there is less patience today with the wider and softer focus that might be needed to recognise spirituality. So, whilst deep and meaningful statements on spirituality do exist, they rarely have the impact and value they deserve.

In recent years spiritual education has been largely ignored in favour of this more acquisitive approach to skills and knowledge. Spirituality often remains as a notional component of a mission statement and only occasionally breaks into the curriculum. In some schools it has been consigned completely to the RE department in a way that seems to absolve other departments from engaging with spirituality at all. Even in the less formal settings of youth work, the spiritual dimension has been viewed with suspicion as a kind of imposition or even an indoctrination of young people. In this climate, the leader in a Christian community needs to be clear about how spirituality might appear in general and how it should be recognised and celebrated in the curriculum of school and youth work.

---

14 *Promoting and evaluating pupils' spiritual, moral, social and cultural development HMI 2125 2004*

15 *National Occupational Standards for Youth Work. PAULO 2002 see especially section B2*

The spiritual lives of the young

Young people lead rich and varied spiritual lives. They are caught up in a process of rapid growth in bodily change, relationships and self-awareness. On a daily basis, young people are exploring the mystery of who they are and their relationship to the world around them. Openness, frustration, questions, gratitude and wonder litter their day. Virtues are being forged in the heat of arguments and in the confusion of choices. Self-sacrifice is being practised in every playground and in every youth club, every day. This implicit spirituality is the holy ground on which all education takes place. It is the spirit that drives young people to learn, to respect others and to value their interior life and guard it from exploitation. The spiritual dimension is brought into a sharper focus from time to time but usually it operates in soft focus and may even be suppressed in settings that are unsafe for its expression. A secular culture will tend to establish a taboo about talking spiritually. It makes spiritual and religious experience a private and undervalued aspect of living. The task of the leader, in a Christian community, is to recognise and celebrate the submerged spiritual dimension appropriately, recognising that for adolescents in particular it is a shy and vulnerable aspect of their experience. Creating safe spaces for spirituality to find expression and flourish is a key task for leadership.

Recognising Spirituality

Recent research by David Hay and Rebecca Nye into the spirituality of young people has identified a core spiritual awareness that has been termed relational consciousness.[16]

This catches two patterns of awareness that come together in a young person, which together move them into a different mode of seeing and thinking that would generally be called spiritual. The two patterns are:

A heightened level of consciousness or perception compared to the normal conversation of the young person.

A concern about relatedness, how things connect between themselves, others, the world and God.

---

16   David Hay & Rebecca Nye *The Spirit of The Child* page 131
      (Jessica Kingsley Publishers 2006)

For Hay and Nye these two elements created a step-change in awareness that gave the young person access to a more holistic view of themselves and their place in the world. It is as if they glimpse a mystery that will never yield to language and touch an energy that motivates the search for meaning. Hay and Nye suggest that each young person has a unique spiritual *signature*, a personal style of accessing the spiritual dimension. Their spirituality needs to be sensed by the adult rather than be defined by some objective criteria. Recognising the spiritual is therefore an intuitive process that operates in a relational context and it is a skill that spiritual leaders need to develop in working with colleagues and young people. Spirituality may emerge in peak moments, in dramatic and tragic situations. For the most part it emerges as a deep background to all of life experience, a barely recognised sacramental awareness of God hidden in the ordinary flow of the day. The flow of the spiritual dimension is discernable in some of the ordinary behaviour of young people. The leader, searching for spirituality in the young, may find the list of Indicators below helpful, in tuning their attention to the spiritual in the ordinary.

Thirty Indicators of spiritual awareness in young people

This is not a check list. The behaviours listed are indicators that something spiritual might be happening in some young people some of the time. The way that different behaviours may coalesce or pattern themselves will vary uniquely in each young person. The list is meant as a stimulus to the awareness of the leader in identifying the spiritual and the sacred moments that are scattered, unspoken through the ordinary exchanges of the day.

Getting carried away with the flow of an activity, being lost in that moment
Persistent curiosity energised from within
Delighting in some discovery or insight
Creative, intensive energy
Acts of self-sacrifice
Choosing silence and stillness
Self-control betraying an inner strength and spirit
Having the courage to ask for forgiveness
Seeing new connections to other knowledge
Habits of virtue, compassion, justice, warmth etc.
Thinking in whole concepts, holistically
Asking meaningful questions

Getting angry about others being damaged
Enjoying ambiguity and paradox
Being caught up in a sense of peace
Being able to reflect under pressure
Awareness of a journey-sense to life
Being caught up in idealism
Hunger to learn and know more
In touch with inner conflicts
Wanting to make a difference to the world
Showing a sense of personal integrity
Expressing gratitude
Being habitually optimistic and cheerful
Respecting all life as precious and connected
Day-dreaming and meditating on life-experience
Aware of feeling strange
Being ready to stay with a particular mood
Being able to focus on the way things relate
Wondering about themselves and the world

This list is meant to stimulate reflection about how the spiritual may be unfolding in young lives. All of the behaviours can have a specific explanation in the context of the school or youth group. Hay and Nye suggest that the quality of the awareness intensifies in these types of behaviour. Hopefully the adults involved will recognise the change of intensity and be ready to encourage and revere what is happening without drawing inappropriate attention to it. If Hay and Nye are correct, then every classroom and youth club is filled with a spiritual activity to which little attention has yet been given by adults. Linking spirituality and the curriculum begins with the recognition that every young person is a spiritual being and that they are behaving spiritually in the learning situation, at least some of the time. Every encounter with young people, each conversation, each question raised and each silence shared is filled with a spiritual potential that needs to be recognised, animated and protected by the adult leader.

In Church-based schools and projects these general behaviours are given a context, a tradition and a language in which they can be shared, celebrated and affirmed. The tradition offers a map and compass for the life journey that values the interior spiritual life and helps people to connect with common language and values at the deepest level. The journey from the unspoken potentially spiritual behaviours listed above to a full Church-based commitment may never be completed by many young people. However, the values, the awareness and the experience of belonging to a spiritual community may be sufficient to support young people throughout their whole life-journey. Each meditative moment shared in groups, each liturgy celebrated in school will affirm the inner life of young people and help them to claim some spiritual energy to share with others. The spirit, that leads us to recognise the source of all mystery as *Father* connects all seeking meaning to the story of Jesus and lends direction and purpose to everything else.

In the classroom this will mean recognising the energy around issues and curriculum content. Being ready to stop and listen to young people, at the level of feelings, will open up spirituality. Listening for intuitive explanations, recognising original links and creativity will encourage young people to value their inner spirit. Such focused listening puts young people in touch with learning as a personal experience rather than an instruction session. Allowing time to explore empathy with others, discovering implications and links with other subjects breaks down the compartmentalised curriculum that seems unnatural to a more holistic approach to learning.

Viewing young people as spiritual, reconnects teachers to the source of their vocational energy. Awareness of that hidden energy allows the teacher or youth worker to bear with the frustrations and thoughtlessness of young people. It gives motivation to engage with young people and maintain a friendly approach. The teacher is caught up in the same spiritual energy that moves in young people and a more holistic view of life can emerge through the teaching vocation. The fact that the same spiritual energy sustains adults and young people, creates an equality that can allow the teaching role to move from adult into the young people. Young people can teach and adults can learn in a more democratic atmosphere when spiritual values are recognised and control and command are less dominant.

Leaders in the Christian community have the subtle and challenging task of raising awareness of the spiritual dimension in the learning environment. This can be done partly through training opportunities but it will only be sustained through good example. The modelling of this awareness in relationships with colleagues is part of the leader's spiritual role. The approach outlined here will be caught rather than taught. It will be helped by small rituals such as a moment of silence or a prayer before classes or group sessions. It will develop more clearly if the adults can introduce their own spiritual experience appropriately. When incidents happen, feelings explode or change happens, there will always be an opportunity for the adult to make a connection between life and the gospel. Celebrations and reconciliations are moments to express gratitude in a prayer or reflection. All these moments help young people to recognise an interior life, a mystery and the sense of connectedness that makes us all spiritual.

Spirituality in Curriculum Areas

Spirituality is a cross-curricular theme. It has an important place in every subject area because the young people involved in learning are all spiritual people. The need to get through core material on the curriculum can often undermine the need to linger on questions and explore the connections with other topics. The desiccated and compartmentalised nature of the national curriculum needs to be viewed holistically from time to time if it is to have a spiritual flavour and a depth that engages with inner meaning. David Hay suggests that educators working spiritually within the curriculum have four major responsibilities:

Helping children to keep an open mind
Exploring ways of seeing
Encouraging personal awareness
Becoming personally aware of the social and political dimensions of spirituality.

The temptation to offer immediate answers to questions is overwhelming in the race to get through material that will be tested later in the school year. The temptation to play the role of an expert rather than an explorer takes away the opportunity for wonder and the chance to struggle to clarify thoughts and connections in education. In exam schemes there is little room for exploring different ways of seeing and making intuitive and personal connections that reinforce self esteem and identity. Giving attention to personal awareness in the learning situation is a skill that needs practice and strategies that rarely emerge in formal teaching. The educator, acting spiritually in a secular culture, needs to be aware of the hidden opportunities and threats to spiritual awareness that may be bundled in with changes to policy and planning for the future.

In each subject area there will be many opportunities to engage the spiritual dimension of life. The PE class, trying to warm up and get focused is only a thought away from the centring process that Christians use as a way in to meditation and prayer. The University of York has recently opened a faculty of Sport and Spirituality at St John's College. The Geography department in my own school recently made an emotional map of the school. The sense of sacred space could equally find room in the Geography curriculum. Mathematics with its patterns and inner beauty is more than just a functional activity for economic gain. Mathematics is taught more effectively if fewer steps are offered to smooth the path to solutions. If the students have to struggle with approaches and with concepts the opportunity for surprise and wonder increases.[17] That need to struggle with ideas, for learning to take place, is demonstrated in the life of Jesus as a teacher: His teaching vehicle was the story, well told, rooted in experience with learning locked into it. In general, Jesus told the story and let the listeners struggle with the meaning. He allowed them to reflect, to question and to wonder and to discover for themselves. In the current sophisticated educational climate such approaches are still relevant for those who wish to be teachers rather than information dispensers.

English language can open up the inner world of imagination and empathy, engage emotion and explore self-expression in ways that are rooted in spiritual living. History, design technology, music, art and information technology all have a capacity to open up questions, meaning and wonder. The teacher's love of a subject area is almost certainly rooted in a spiritual engagement that needs to be shared if their own motivation is to be sustained. Themes such as wonder, questioning, exploring, original thinking, self-expression and mystery, offer possible ways to develop a cross-curricular approach to spiritual education. The child who wonders about the size of the universe in science may, in the next class, be wondering about how to express their deepest hope in English. The young person who is delighted to have spoken confidently in a mathematics class, for the first time ever, may well consolidate the delight in contributing to French. The wonder and the delight were not on the curriculum but in the end they may be far more significant than the French vocabulary and the mathematical formulae in which they were expressed.

Awareness of these spiritual and ordinary moments in the development of young people needs to be part of the stock-in-trade of the Christian leader. Creating cross-curricular projects that highlight spiritual learning can help move the focus from the content to the process of learning and create a more holistic experience for young people. In contemporary culture the inner life of young people is impoverished by a glut of electronic images and a poverty of imagination. Play is less and less an activity and more and more a passive entertainment. One of the tasks of spiritual education is to strengthen the creative, playful spirit that is often damaged by the over-stimulation of a media-filled world. The ability to enjoy thinking, generate new ideas, search

---

17   *Mathematics Education Review* no 11 1999 page 32 Exploring the relationship between wonder and Mathematics.

for answers and explore mystery are all anaesthetised by the remorseless, superficial imagery that holds the attention but leaves no time for reflection.

In that context spiritual education may need to address three cultural wounds identified by Fr Michael Paul Gallagher:[18]

Wounded Memory – The removal of the spiritual from the public domain cutting the connection to traditions and shared values with the past. Religion has retreated into a privatised and individual experience.

Wounded Belonging – Religion and spirituality are seen simply as a way to personal happiness. There is an avoidance of pain and an absence of compassion and the solidarity that makes us human.

Wounded Imagination – So much is imagined for us today, the media have colonised parts of our minds. Imagination is a sacramental way to engage with God and mystery. Sadly it has been devalued in the present culture.

These needs are most obvious in the youngest and most vulnerable members of the population. Education, if it is to lead to life, must address these needs. In responding to wounded memory, Church-based communities can bring young people the traditions and symbols that link them to a story. In meeting the need to belong, we must address the individualism that will not accept the need to support others. Justice and service events created, executed and celebrated by the community can strengthen a sense of shared identity and belonging. In meeting the challenge of a devalued imagination the Church can offer a sacramental view of the whole of life as a sign of God's presence immediately experienced by each person. The awareness that imagination brings of God, as present in one's own life, is the doorstep of faith and a source of real energy for living. If imagination is seen simply as a fleeting fantasy then the reality and the energy it offers are missed.

Classrooms are settings where a spiritual curriculum is being worked through, albeit unconsciously. Wonder, awe, fascination, curiosity, self-sacrifice, empathy and stillness lie just below the surface in every lesson. The task of the spiritual leader is to raise awareness of this deeper and eternal curriculum flowing beneath the sometimes fickle trends of bureaucratic change that seem to ruffle more than the surface of school and youth projects. The wise leader

---

18 Address at Ushaw College Durham July 25th 2006. The titles are from the talk, the comments are the author's own notes.

will ensure that they have some time to reflect on the spiritual dimension of their work. They will find that such reflection puts them in touch with that spiritual compass that draws them towards life-giving choices. They will find in the gospel both strength and direction in planning and uniting colleagues in a community approach to spiritual education.

Questions

Which young people in your setting would you describe as spiritually aware? What evidence do you have for that judgment?

How easy is it to move from information-sharing to inspiration-sharing, in your work with colleagues and young people?

How can you create space for imagination and exploration in work with colleagues and young people?

How can safe opportunities be provided for colleagues and young people to share their experience of awe, wonder, belonging and brokenness?

What kind of whole school or group activities might be developed to stimulate some visible holistic dimension to community life?

Reflection

With doodles and daydreams,
When a child should be learning,
God sets the mind free,
Feeds deeper yearnings.

Time can stand still,
Imagination soar,
The creative spirit slips
Through sense's doors.

Each subject has doorways
To wonder and awe,
Landing a child
On a spiritual shore.

Doorways in numbers,
In language and story,
Open young minds
To intimate glory.

In training for rounders,
Or when there's a goal,
The doors of eternity
Swing wide for the soul.

In the heart of each child,
Whatever the lesson,
Is a springboard to mystery
Splash! What a blessing!

CHAPTER 8

THE LEADER AS GOOD SHEPHERD

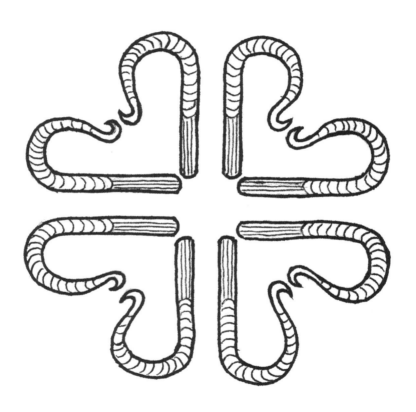

Jesus compares himself to a good shepherd in the gospel of Saint John. Using images that would have been familiar to all his listeners he describes the skill of the good shepherd and the shepherd's relationship with the sheep. The shepherd is described as:

Knowing the sheep individually
Having a detailed knowledge of the country
Vigilant in watching for wolves and other threats
Creating sheepfolds, safe places for the sheep
Laying down his life when needed
Open to other sheep joining the flock
Constantly moving to new pasture

These images, rooted in a rural landscape, take on a new significance when viewed in the context of leadership in schools and youth groups today. There are no wolves stalking school corridors and no lack of water and food for young people. Pessimism however, bullying and sadness roam many corridors and even set up home in the hearts of young people and colleagues. The aching in hearts is less likely to be a hunger for bread and more likely to be a hunger for recognition and reassurance. Awareness of these individual needs and the ability to protect, guide and lead people to life are the qualities of a good shepherd. In using these gifts, leaders will find themselves entering the mind of Jesus as they work professionally and genuinely with the young.

Knowing the sheep individually

The shepherd in Jesus' model knows the sheep by name. They are individuals. The personal dimension, being known, recognised and named is a transforming experience, especially for young people. Remembering names is a challenge, especially in large schools. When the quality of conversation improves, people are listened to and hearts can be changed. Remembering a birthday of a colleague, or the fact that they have a fear of heights on a trip to the mountains can reassure them and strengthen them for the challenge. A word in the ear to a young person to check if they have got over an illness or an argument can have an electrifying effect on the individual relationship. The sense of being remembered, recognised and understood opens up healthy relationships that allow confidence to grow. In time, the leader will be trusted by the individual with opportunities for personal guidance and be allowed to be an educator not just in the classroom but in the hearts of others.

The range of people a leader can know individually is limited not only by numbers but also by personality and prejudice. Introvert young people will generally find it easier to connect with introvert leaders. Extrovert and loud young people will tend to be drawn to outgoing and boisterous adults. There are young people and colleagues that some leaders will never successfully engage with, even if they know them well. Sometimes prejudice can block personal engagement. An adult who has had a poor experience from leadership over many years may have a suspicion of management that effectively closes off anything but a cool professional relationship. A pupil who has inherited a degree of racial prejudice from their home may be out of reach initially from ethnic staff in school. In one sense *the flock chooses the shepherd* since the power to engage or not to engage ultimately lies in the heart of the young person or the colleague involved. Therefore each leader, working to shepherd life in a school community will find a sphere of influence that takes in some people and not others. There will be some people who will open their heart to a leader and some who never will, a flock who will listen and others who never will. In commenting on this phenomenon Don Bosco advised that when disciplining a person it was often more effective to find some friendly adult to have a quiet word than to use someone with whom the person had no positive relationship. Each leader will have their own sphere of influence, a flock that hears them and recognises their voice. The danger is that some young people and colleagues will not have any sense of belonging or feel recognised by the adult leaders. These are the lost sheep that need to be searched out, celebrated and connected to positive relationships in the Christian community.

Having a detailed knowledge of the country

I remember talking to an experienced teacher about my concern for the morale in a school. People were moaning, punctuality was poor and energy was low. The teacher replied with great certainty that this would all disappear in another two weeks. He explained that a dip in energy always happened at that time of year for pupils and for staff. He was not concerned at all because he knew the landscape of the school year. Whilst others were reading timetables, this teacher had been reading the emotional map of the school and knew its peak moments, its featureless plateaux and its valleys of darkness. Knowing the landscape meant he could offer reassurance, encourage and energise when others could not see a wider horizon and were losing heart.

The shepherds' knowledge comes from experience not just map-reading. They know, because they have been there before. They have lived the highs and lows, alongside young people. They have remembered, reflected and grown through their experience. It is not enough to have lived the experience; the shepherd must assimilate the wisdom that comes from reflection. That wisdom is triggered not just by predictable moments in a working year but also by the emotional impact and issues presented by both colleagues and young people. As a young youth worker I was overwhelmed by the responsibility of hearing a young person's grief shared after years of silence. In that new situation, I needed a guide to place this experience into the wider context. I was shepherded through a sensitive area by an older and wiser leader and in the process I grew in experience, the young person was helped and I had found a wise guide for future problems.

Christian thinking suggests that God speaks to us through what happens. That means that all of life is worth reflecting upon. In the busy timetabled flow of each day it is difficult to reflect, to step back and look for meaning and guidance. Don Bosco challenged his staff to become *contemplatives in action:* able to keep part of their awareness on a deeper and more spiritual dimension of daily living. A leader who shepherds life will feel the tug of a deeper spirit within themselves as they work with others. They become a place where action and spirit flow together in an awareness that brings a deeper wisdom to daily choices.

Vigilant in watching for wolves and other threats

A shepherd develops a sixth sense of awareness when trouble is looming. The shepherd also reads the behaviour of the sheep to identify anxiety, fear and aggression. Vigilance implies that the shepherd never really sleeps. Like a parent listening for young children, part of their awareness is always engaged. The leader, as a shepherd among the young, needs to use imagination to anticipate what might go wrong and be ready to identify a threat before it becomes a problem.

Vigilance extends to all areas of leadership, from counting young people onto coaches on trips, a very shepherd-like activity, to ensuring that the least popular person is not left to the end when choosing teams. Vigilance is a key skill in working with colleagues. Noticing the changes in attitude and in normal working practice and looking for possible reasons behind such changes can help a leader to see threats to team members even before they are aware of them. Recognising destructive moods, comments and body language in colleagues and young people can offer clues to the shepherding leader about how and when to encourage, guide and confront others in the team.

Threats to colleagues or young people are not always predictable. Even experienced leaders need to be vigilant. The advent of the mobile phone, chat rooms and internet downloads have opened up new areas for vigilance that were unknown a decade ago. The affordability of drugs and the culture of binge-drinking create another type of threat that constantly changes its way of approaching young lives. Vigilance extends to maintaining an awareness of what is happening in the world of the young, from music to magazines and from family breakdown to football teams. A good shepherd knows when something new has entered the world of the young, recognises its goodness and guards against the dangers it may bring. Part of this vigilance is achieved simply by talking to the young, showing an interest in what they find attractive. The young educate the leader about their own world so that presence among young people is a vital part of vigilance. The awareness of threats to young people will often arise in conversation between concerned adults and young people. Those conversations will only happen if trust and care are already established. Vigilance is rooted, ultimately, in the friendly presence of adults among the young; not as a policing exercise but rather as the presence of older brothers and sisters, who have a duty of care.

Creating sheepfolds, safe places for the sheep

The circular walls of stone on hill farms, in some countries, are the sheepfolds that protected the sheep at night. They were the safe places where the sheep could share warmth and rest. The image of the sheepfold is significant for educators because the groups and institutions they organise need to be places where young people can feel safe, explore their strengths, make mistakes and grow strong in their self-worth and identity. Don Bosco said that he would guarantee that any young person entering his projects would not get any worse. He felt that if he could not say that then he had no right to open his doors to young people. Such a minimal statement highlights the importance of safety in dealing with young people, all of whom are vulnerable as they explore who they are during their formative years.

At a time when bureaucracy abounds, it is easy to dismiss all procedures and documents as of little value. The shepherding leader however needs to take particular notice of the demands of safety and child protection, in their leadership role. Such concern has a spiritual as well as a procedural dimension in serving the needs of the young. Clarity about recruitment, procedures for risk assessment, protocols about how and when staff talk individually with young people are not optional but crucial for a leader, following the example of the good shepherd. In our culture these are the walls and the gateway of the sheepfold within which the safety of young people is ensured. The good shepherd spends time building, repairing and extending these walls as need requires. In a similar way, the leader identifies lapses in good practice, sees gaps in provision and opens up new ways of ensuring the safety of young people.

Safety involves more than just policy and procedures for the leader who is shepherding life in the Christian community. The emotional atmosphere also needs to be safe. Each relationship and group is a place where safety can lead to life or to setbacks and damage. A young person, risking taking a lead in a conversation or group project needs to know that they will not be ridiculed if they fail. A colleague, exploring a new approach with challenging young people will need to know that they will be supported through any negative feedback. Wherever a personal risk is taken for life and growth the leader needs to build an atmosphere of optimism and personal support as a kind of safety net. The leader also needs to tailor the risk to the experience of the person concerned. A young person with no organisational experience would not be encouraged to run a youth concert in the area as a first step. They might be encouraged to organise the ticketing for such an event. At times, the leader will need to protect some people from an over-estimation of their own abilities.

At the heart of safety is the awareness that each person, young or old, is a child of God with a unique relationship to God that is precious, eternal and yet vulnerable. In working with child protection and guiding young people to steady growth, the leader is protecting and guiding the image of God emerging in others. This is more than following procedures; it is touching the face of God and living a vocation that plumbs the depth of all creation. The leader who creates safety makes a holy space where life can grow. That safe place can expand as the experience and age of young people increases. Measured risks can be taken but safety cannot be forgotten if leaders are to be faithful shepherds of the spirit living in people.

Laying down one's life when needed

Working with young people is not just another job. The dimensions of the task spread beyond the boundaries of any job-description, into the personal mystery of a vocation. The leader especially will experience many times when they are drawn into going *the extra mile* and reaching out beyond what is normally expected, in order to help growth or to minimise damage. This sense of being drawn to self-sacrifice is part of the role of leader's as shepherds, that takes them beyond their formal role into a kind of service that cannot be demanded but can only be freely offered. It is the kind of generous loving that is instinctive and rooted in respect for the value of others.

As a fourteen year old I witnessed a fight between two girls at the bus stop after school. The usual crowd formed to watch but they were horrified when the girls both produced long and sharp aluminium combs that were deadly. Both year eleven girls were strong, tall and out of control. No one dared to intervene. Except a small and quiet female member of staff who was driving past in her car. She stood between them, somehow disarmed them both and asked others to separate them until they calmed down. I had always seen her as diffident character and was amazed at her courage. In one sense she was exercising a duty of care expected of any educator. In another sense, she could easily have driven past and chosen not to see what was happening. She took a personal risk for the safety of others; she was prepared to lay down her life. How many vocations to service were awakened in young people in the crowd around that fight at the bus stop? How many hearts gained courage to do the right thing through that teacher taking the risk of serving the young?

There are other less dramatic ways in which leaders lay down their lives for others. Just keeping the office door open invites the kind of interruptions that meet others' needs. The time lost in work has to be made up later, after school, a sacrifice hidden from others' awareness, but known to God. The leader who calls a colleague at home after a bereavement or illness does not need to do that. The readiness to cover someone else's work for a time is not usually part of a job description but it has to be done and life again is laid down for the sake of young people.

In Jesus' words about shepherding, the good shepherd is contrasted with the hireling who has no real care for the sheep. The motivation of the hireling is simply money. For the good shepherd, the relational dimension is at least as important. The emergence of self-sacrifice is a sign of a deeper sense of vocation in those who work with the young. When a leader sees such sacrifice in others it needs to be quietly affirmed and never taken for granted. Many adults working with the young begin with a generosity and self-sacrifice that is quickly taken for granted and eventually lost through disappointment and cynicism. The leader has the task of shepherding that generous spirit and recognising this precious gift, to the team and to young people.

Open to other sheep joining the flock

Every leader likes a settled team, one that is used to working together and at ease with the differences in personality and giftedness. A team takes time to perform consistently and a stable core is needed for continuity of service for young people. But stability has the danger of stagnation built into it. Comfort is not an effective basis for serving the changing needs of young people. New members need to arrive on a regular basis in the shape of young people and adults if the team is to be fresh and open to change. For the leader as a good shepherd the arrival of new people is a signal from God that the work needs to change or to expand. Sometimes the team itself may recognise a lack of energy or gifts that leads them to recruit new members; that, too, is a signal from God to be open to new horizons.

In work with the young, the leader needs to keep a wider view of the whole community and its needs. Small groups that have worked together for long periods can easily slip into cliques unless others join. Adults who cover specific voluntary tasks in a school or community can be seen to be an exclusive group closed to new volunteers. When groups are closed for long periods they can tend to run out of energy, meet group-needs before task-needs and be slow to recognise when change is due. The leader needs to encourage an open atmosphere and challenge most informal groups to vary their membership on a regular basis.

The same principle applies to groups of young people. Small youth-groups that run parish liturgies are often seen as taking over when they are closed to new membership. School-based voluntary groups, working with prayer or justice issues, are often written off as *do-gooders*. These kinds of comments express a sense of being excluded that needs to be challenged. Small groups formed with young people should be set up with a clear time-scale and with options to continue or drop out and at the same time to offer spaces for new membership.

On a wider scale, a Christian community needs to review its relationship with the local area and the needs of people further afield. It is not the role of a Christian community to be a cosy club that serves the needs of its members. The Christian community is called to make the gospel present in its own time and place. As the times and people change, new groups may need to be formed: new needs will emerge. Simply serving the needs within the Christian community is not sufficient in the following of the gospel. Therefore, a Christian community needs to make a regular review of the needs to which it can respond, beyond its own immediate area. It needs to be open to the new challenges from the sheep that are not yet part of the flock.

Constantly moving to new pastures

Planning meetings across the world reverberate to the phrase *we always do it this way!* There is efficiency and even a comfort in following tried and tested ways of working. The routines and patterns provide a short-hand that allows events and responsibilities to become embedded into a predictable level of commitment for a wide range of people. The disco that always happens two weeks before Christmas can be pencilled-in every year, organised clearly and recognised as a valued part of the programme. The staff event in summer can be anticipated and its date guarded long after the need for it has ceased to exist. Tried and tested events easily change into trying and testy events, endured rather than celebrated, especially in work with young people where needs change faster than adults can adapt. There is an asceticism of change built into youth ministry that challenges adults to return time and time again to listen to the needs of the young and then move towards the resources that will meet those needs. Like a shepherd the adult leader is called to lead young people to new pastures. These new pastures are unavailable if there is no chance to reassess young people's own needs. Listening to the needs is only helpful if the adult knows from experience, reflection and research about how to meet those needs in new ways.

This is not good news for adults who prefer to meet needs with tried and trusted approaches. It is even less attractive news at a time when rapid change is being imposed by central government on schools and youth work in England and Wales. There is a limit to the amount of change that teams and institutions can manage and some people feel that such limits have been exceeded. Too much change generates stress and creates uncertainty. Even young people benefit from predictable routines and clear boundaries if they are to grow into healthy individuals and citizens.

The shepherding analogy of seeking new pastures makes change dependent upon the hunger of the sheep. When things are going well it is important not to change, but when the sheep become restless as pastures are over-grazed, the shepherd knows where to take the sheep next. So change is based on felt needs and does not happen for its own sake and certainly not because the shepherd needs a change. This needs-led approach to change is another aspect of listening and discernment in the adult teams that work with the young. It is motivated from within the group of adults and young people and not an arbitrary imposition from outside. Change like this tends to energise adults and sharpen their focus and team work in the service of the young. Rather than being resented it is embraced as the will of a community that serves the young and it mobilises change rather than prescribing it in documentation.

Change in youth work and even formal education is generated by the felt needs of young people, the resources available and the focused energy of the adults to bridge needs and resources. There will always be a tension between standing in a traditional pattern and responding to immediate needs. There is a constant need in shepherding young lives to listen to needs and develop new resources. It could be that reviewing needs simply leads to a confirmation that the team are in the right place, doing the right thing at the right time. Such a confirmation of the relevance of the present pattern affirms the tradition developing in the work but it also roots it in present needs, rather than in assumptions from the past.

The shepherd does not have a fixed home but lives a nomadic existence moving with the sheep. The leader of young people shares that nomadic existence and has a role that is based in relationships rather than in a place or a pattern of working. The relationship is with young people and with the mystery of God within. Each plan and pattern of working needs to revolve around those two key relationships as a touchstone, a compass that guides the leader through change and towards new pastures as and when they are needed.

Questions

Take each of the characteristics listed below and describe how you manage these shepherding tasks in your own setting.

Knowing young people individually

Having a detailed knowledge of their background and needs

Vigilance in watching for danger

Creating safe places for the young and vulnerable

Readiness for self sacrifice and support

Openness to others – avoiding unhealthy cliques

Inspiring and managing change at the right time

What would you identify as the main threats to the well being of a) the adults and b) the young people in your context?

Where would you like your flock, your community, to be in three years time?

Jesus described the good shepherd as one who was prepared to lay down his life and take risks and make sacrifices. Are there limits to the amount of extra work and self sacrifice a leader might take on?

Reflection

The shepherd knows them all by name,
Each one has its place.
In the shepherd's heart,
They are recognised with grace.

The shepherd knows the danger,
Before it can do harm,
By guiding and distracting sheep
To life and peace and calm.

The shepherd welcomes others,
To come in from the cold.
Creating room for each of them
To shelter in the fold.

The shepherd stays awake at night,
To watch for those who stray,
And in the darkness and the storm,
The shepherd tries to pray.

The flock will need to move along
To greener grass and streams.
There is no long-term resting place,
For the shepherd or their dreams.

So in the service of the sheep,
The shepherd spends his day,
Pouring life and love into
A living gospel way.

CHAPTER 9

CARING FOR CARERS

One of the key tasks of leadership in a Christian community is to care for those who work with and for the young. Guiding and educating young adolescents will always carry a large element of personal challenge as boundaries are tested and emotions rise and fall among the young. Managing the stress that such a setting might generate in colleagues is part of the leader's task in supporting healthy adult teams. Anyone who undertakes a role working with adolescents has to accept that there will be stressful times; when emotions are unfairly targeted at the adult by young people, times when peer-pressure leads to inappropriate behaviour, and parental expectations are unrealistic and expressed aggressively.

Most professional organisations recognise the duty of care a leader carries for the adult team. There will often be an array of support through advice, referral and other resources of which the leader will need to be aware. The ability to match the needs of colleagues to such support is a skill to be developed by a leader in any organisation. In a Christian community however, the available resources are increased to include the spirituality and tradition of the Church. The leader's own relationship with the adult team is also extended into a spiritual dimension not normally expected in secular settings. The purpose of this chapter is to explore the spiritual dimension of care for leaders in a Christian community. None of the suggestions below are meant to substitute for the practical support of colleagues in the work place. Instead they are meant to provide a richer context and wider resources to help the leader to support other adults to explore their own spiritual journey and to remain in touch with the personal energy of their vocation to work with the young.

Recognition

It seems such a simple thing to smile, to say someone's name or to offer a brief word of appreciation. Yet the impact of such brief acts of recognition can warm and sustain other adults on the team for the rest of the day. It is not simply a matter of recognising faces and saying names; it is also recognising the story behind each face and the particular challenges, triumphs and disasters that they may carry in their work with the young. The short moment of recognition, the nod on a corridor and the quiet word of thanks, become shorthand connections to the inner spiritual life of colleagues. These moments are the visible expressions of a deeper recognition of a common vocation to work with the young and an appreciation of the kind of dedication and sacrifice that such work involves.

Recognition is the cumulative expression of previous conversations and observation by the leader. The teacher, having all their assessments complete when the leader knows that they have been ill, needs recognition. The newly-appointed youth worker who maintains patience with young people who are being aggressive, needs support and affirmation from the team leader. Recognition needs to be personal. It is built on the leader's awareness of the strengths and weaknesses of the team and it is best done quietly and often, rather than publicly and rarely. The challenge for the leader lies in knowing the team and seeing things from their perspective, noticing where they falter, how they cope with success and how they manage setbacks. When the leader is able to see the challenges, fears and hopes of colleagues, then their smaller triumphs and disappointments are more easily recognised and a sense of community can be built at a vocational level.

Recognition demands that the leader moves the centre of their thinking from themselves to others. This move towards selflessness is part of the leader's spiritual journey; a self-emptying that is seen as crucial to spiritual growth in every religious tradition. The ability to keep one's own concerns in perspective and allow others to develop and succeed, is part of the maturity that spiritual leadership demands. It is part of the role of being a good shepherd; knowing the sheep and helping them to grow to fullness of life as individuals.

Using Spiritual Language

In a Christian community, events do not happen in a vacuum but rather in a landscape that has a specific shape and meaning. The leader who cares spiritually for other colleagues needs to be aware of the spiritual landscape within which those other adults may be moving. Some may be very positive and confident in their work, others less so. Some may be burdened with worries or weakened by lack of confidence. Some others may tend to overstretch themselves and others may never take the risk of doing more. In each case the language of the gospel: the need for both Cross and Resurrection will speak in different ways. The language of a spiritual journey and the idea of being a pilgrim through life will mean different things depending if one is confident or anxious. The leader needs to reflect spiritually on the way that life is unfolding for members of the team and offer spiritual images and language that can take them back to the vocational energy that alone can sustain them.

The image of the good shepherd, for example, can make a lot of sense to a teacher who is aiming to get control of class groups early in their career. It takes the task of guidance, boundaries and control away from a simply a mechanical task or an *ego-issue* and connects it to a deeper energy to protect and nurture. Using that image to describe the situation can help sustain the teacher spiritually and protect their vocation from disappointment and frustration. The Christian story sees failure as part of a bigger picture, part of a journey and not a disaster or a dead end. In supporting colleagues the leader, acting spiritually, can draw on gospel stories of talents, storms, feeding the hungry, crosses and empty tombs. These stories open up an inner landscape that can give meaning to the day-to-day struggles of all members of a Christian community. In the Christian tradition, the Eucharist, with its emphasis on growth through brokenness and community, can offer meaning and a sense of belonging that goes beyond all words and into the mystery of a vocation to work with the young.

The use of such imagery, the promise to pray for colleagues and the ability to link their lives to the gospel landscape can offer a care and guidance that enhances and underpins the normal levels of colleague support available. Such language needs to be introduced sensitively and at the right moment. Often it can be introduced as the way that the Christian tradition might see the situation of a team member. It is not an opportunity to preach at colleagues or to proselytise them. It is a genuine attempt to access the ethos of the community and use it for the benefit of the adults as well as the young people. In many cases, the spiritual dimension cannot be articulated at all by the leader. Even then it has a power to explain, to enlighten and to strengthen the confidence of the leader to guide and encourage the team member with whom they are working. Much of Christian spirituality is better lived out than spoken out. It is only after it has been lived that it can be really heard by others.

Celebrations

Getting together with colleagues to waste a little time together is a prophetic act on the part of leadership. It is a recognition that there is a wider perspective that makes sense of what we are doing. The remorseless pressure of targets, tests and evaluation can give the impression that the adults are entirely responsible for whatever is seen as success or failure in work for the young. Celebrations recognise a deeper mesh of meaning and quietly recognise the cost of being with young people. The celebration is not a reward for work well done but is instead the feeding of the spirit that holds people together in the service of the young. It is not an occasional option but a regular way that leadership can serve the teams they lead.

Don Bosco spoke about the need to step beyond the roles we carry and into a friendly presence with others. Celebrations bridge and break down the roles that can sometimes divide and replace them with a lively spirit of confidence. Nights-out, quizzes, staff choirs and gatherings after work, all help to build relationships that model positive adult roles to young people. The science department in one school has a Friday cake session for all their staff, including the technicians. Those few moments once a week have been a foundation for good teamwork, calmer classes and tighter waistbands! Celebrations need little excuse because for Christians there is always a reason to celebrate. We believe in a God who can turn tragedy to new life, and death into an eternal belonging. So every celebration is an act of faith in life whilst it is still imperfect, unfinished and even confusing. When in doubt, celebrate!

Births Marriages and Deaths

Opportunities to care and to celebrate are provided by life events that will touch adult lives on a regular basis. Leaders need to recognise the chance to focus on people rather than their roles through births, sickness, marriages, bereavements and other life-changing moments. A quiet mention of a colleague's struggle and an invitation to prayer at a staff meeting or a quiet word in the ear can lift the heart of that person and draw the community more closely around them for a while. The ability to celebrate new life and love among colleagues lightens the pressures of work and lifts the spirit of the teams they work with. One youth project, realising that two of the team had married just a year before, decided to re-enact the marriage and created a reception afterwards with speeches and presents. It was a spontaneous way to celebrate the couple and the community and had a huge impact on the life of the group. Anniversaries of joy and sadness, sensitively recalled by leaders, can help weave the stories of staff and the community into a more supportive embrace. In that atmosphere, hearts can be opened and needs made known in a way that draws the whole community deeper into the mystery of life, death and resurrection.

Welcoming the Stranger

Most spiritual traditions place strong emphasis not on *stranger danger* but on welcoming the stranger. The story of two disciples walking to Emmaus after the death of Jesus is just one way that the theme is found in Christianity. The disciples welcomed a stranger and found that they were walking with Jesus. In the process they found that their hearts were on fire with new insight and energy for the future. In working with the young as adults, this tradition suggests a special care for new staff and volunteers. Taking time to introduce new staff to others, to explain how things work, where to go for help, and making the first move in saying *Hello* become, for the Christian, acts of loving-kindness and not simply good professional practice.

In Christian communities, new arrivals bring a fresh sense of God's presence into the teams they work with. They bring a new experience and background that upsets the pattern of existing relationships. They bring needs that draw new strengths from long-established staff and they offer the precious gift of first impressions and insights that may have escaped the long-term workers on the team. Welcoming the stranger is therefore an act of loving-kindness for the new arrival but also a part of the enrichment of the adult team for the future. It is a way of drawing down a blessing on everyone, a way of caring for the carers.

The Limitations of Care

There are some boundaries about caring for the carers which need to be recognised, even if they are crossed occasionally. Not all the needs that adults bring to their work can be or should be met within that setting. In Christian teamwork people are called to work together for others in the spirit of the gospel. Sometimes an individual's needs are so great that they can no longer continue to be effective in their work. It is not the task of the leaders to become counsellors, substitute families or a safety-net for all the needs of the team they lead.

This is particularly difficult for the many heart-led leaders in Christian communities. The initial instinct for compassion and support of needy staff is entirely proper, but the tendency to be drawn into complex, extended personal needs may well develop an unhealthy dependency. Many Christian leaders, in my own experience, suffer from the *disease to please*, making them easy to manipulate at times. Caring for the carers in that setting means that other team members may need to rescue a leader from getting too embroiled in needs that have little to do with the main task of serving the young.

In spiritual terms each person has a cross to carry. In caring for the carers it is important that they carry their own cross, it is their problem and burden and there are limits to the responsibility we carry for others. We cannot get onto another person's cross even though we may stand by and recognise their struggle. We are, as Archbishop Romero said, *ministers, not messiahs.* We do not need to have all the answers or meet every need.

Creating an Environment of Care

Don Bosco built a caring community for young people that involved creating a home, a school, a playground and a church, in city-centre Turin. That model has grown into a spirituality of care that identifies four ways of caring as a community for the needs of all, including the adults.

Belonging
Learning
Relaxing
Meaning

The experience of Don Bosco led him to believe that keeping this fourfold balance led to an environment in which everyone could grow, including the adults. It was a community of gospel life, based on an optimistic humanism that set people free to be themselves in community. This fourfold pattern could become a checklist for care in the school or youth-group.[19]

---

19 More details about this approach can be found in the introduction
    to *Ordinary Ways* referenced at the back of this book.

Questions

How far do people feel they belong?

How warm are relationships between staff? How quickly are disputes resolved? What is body-language like in staff rooms and meetings? Is there evidence that people feel supported and part of something bigger?

Is learning happening for everyone?

Is ongoing training being offered regularly and evenly for staff and volunteers? Do adults have time to reflect on experience and share good practice? Are good resources, reading and presentations available and shared? Do team-members have a chance to share ideas beyond their immediate group? Is there a realistic budget allocated to development of the whole staff? When critical incidents occur, does the community take the opportunity of the learning involved and develop? Are there gifts and talents in staff that are ignored or under-used?

Are opportunities to relax given space & encouragement?

Don Bosco used music, drama and sport to build relaxation into young lives. How many sporting activities happen for staff? What opportunities are there for staff to engage a wider range of gifts and activities with one another? When did you last hear extended laughter from a group of staff? Is there evidence of mature friendships among staff? Are facilities available for staff to use when the young people have gone? Is there a social budget to encourage events for staff? Are the staff-areas welcoming and comfortable?

Is the dimension of meaning and vocation given space to grow?

In a secular age it is easy to overlook the importance of meaning and motivation in sustaining the vocation to work with the young. Are there good start-up programmes and prayers that awaken this dimension in staff? Are resources available to sustain the spiritual life of adults? Are there elements of work with the young that offer opportunities to promote the vocational dimension of teachers and youth workers? Are there symbols and reminders of the spiritual in the meeting-rooms and corridors? Are links made to other agencies that can sustain the spiritual through visits? Do prayer-experiences and retreats happen just for staff?

Good youth-work and education is about relationships and not first of all about delivering a product or gaining an outcome. Most of the growth and learning that happens in schools and youth-settings is a matter of the heart, immeasurable and invaluable for the lives of the young. Sustaining the adult team with life-giving spiritual health is the foundation of all the rest of the work. We do not learn or grow to be human on our own but only in community. Care for the adults not only sustains them for the task of dealing with inconsistent and often thankless youth; it is also a way of modelling positive adult-roles for the future and an act of faith and of friendship for the young.

CHAPTER 10

JOY, OPTIMISM & CHEERFULNESS IN LEADERSHIP.

It is no coincidence that some of the most effective leaders I have ever met go to work most days with a spring in their step and talk easily about loving the job that they do. They tend to focus on what needs to be done and hold back, at least in public, from bewailing the problems they must face. This energy and zest is part of the vocation to leadership. It suggests a joy and buoyancy of spirit that, whilst it may not be permanent is still the prevalent way in which that person encounters life. Such giftedness is not always held by the cleverest or most experienced members of a team, it can emerge in quiet or younger team members as the vital element that carries a team forward. If the named leaders do not feel that kind of enthusiasm and buoyancy it is important for them to identify where it may be found in the team and also to know how to maintain their own buoyancy of spirit within the call to leadership.

The importance of leading with joy and optimism is caught briefly in this quote from Baden Powell, talking about leadership:

> **Your natural inclination is to preach and to warn other travellers of snags in the path, but isn't it better to signal to them some of the joys by the way which they might otherwise miss?**

One of the roles of leaders is not simply to find joy and optimism in their own life but to awaken that joy in others as a sustaining inner energy for life. Buddhist philosophy identifies joy as one of the seven factors in awakening and it is undoubtedly part of the leader's role to awaken that love for life in others. Without that enlivening and visionary hope the leader becomes a manager of things rather than an inspirer of people.

Joy as a sign of vocation

A common delusion promoted by the consumer culture is that we cannot be happy without another television channel, wardrobe item, or holiday. The delusion lies in the suggestion that our deepest happiness depends upon something beyond us. Consumerism makes our happiness dependent upon possessions and experiences which have to be purchased. When our basic needs for food and shelter have been met such links between possessions and happiness seem very superficial. In many situations it is we who choose to be happy or to be sad. The decision is made when we focus predominantly on problems or on what is positive in our living.

Leaders are always at risk of sliding their focus towards the problem-centred end of the spectrum of life. Meetings and emergencies are usually focused around something or someone who is not working well, so the leader's view is constantly populated with problems. The energy to meet these setbacks with buoyancy and optimism comes from a wider view of the situation and a deeper sense of being called to solve problems on the way to a bigger vision. A leader, sat in the third problem-centred meeting of the day in a school, needs to be reminded that whilst three people may have caused a crisis there are perhaps over a thousand others in the school who are happily getting on with life. Leaders who focus solely on problems will lose the stamina that comes from a grateful heart and a wider vision.

When I wake up in the morning I think of what a precious privilege it is to be alive, to breathe, to think and to love!

Those words of the Emperor Marcus Aurelius almost 2000 years ago catch the energy of a leader who could count his blessings. Sometimes the counting of blessing may not take a leader very long, but there will always be a positive somewhere to feed the inner spirit on the sometimes lonely road of leadership. It may simply be a conversation with a child that reminds a leader of the goodness of young people. It may be a moment of peace before a meeting when the leader realises that, despite all the problems, they have been called personally to make a difference to the teams they work with. For other leaders, there may be a very clear guiding-vision that burns quietly within them and helps them to keep moving forward, whatever obstacles they might have to meet. One of the disciplines of leadership might just be to lie in bed at the end of a day and count the blessings they may have missed and quietly thank God for each of them. The result will be a raised awareness of God's presence walking with them and easing the yoke of leadership minute by minute in the working day. The scriptural roots of such an approach can be found in Philippians 4: 4-9 in which Saint Paul links happiness to a focus on whatever is good, true and worthy of praise.

The vocational compass of leaders, therefore, needs to have a needle that points to inner joy in the work that they are doing. That joy does not depend upon everything going well but rather that they are in the right place, doing their best with the gifts they have been given. Joseph Campbell, the well-known anthropologist, described this sense of an inner compass as *following your bliss*. It describes something much deeper than success and catches something of an engagement with an inner gift and call. It evokes a wider vision and a cause that may sometimes lead to a struggle and perhaps to the deepest joys that come through hardships that will give meaning and significance to one's whole life story. For Christians, that dynamic of being challenged through gifts and awareness to build a better world is called the Way of the Cross, a partnership with Jesus that leads to eternal significance and life.

Optimism – as a leadership virtue

Don Bosco advised those who work with the young to avoid bewailing the present times and glorifying the past. Instead he challenged his co-workers to identify good things that appeal to the young and build on them. Focusing and fanning the embers of joy in young lives is a way to energise their spirit to grow in a balanced way through success and the lessons of failure. The same is true of colleagues who also need to be reminded of the positive and to be grounded in real gratitude by wise leadership. Joy and optimism are self-propagating and constantly in a battle with sadness and failure for the hearts of young people and those who work with them. In this battle, adults must lead by example every day and sow the seeds of hope through regular praise, hospitable smiles and celebrations. Leadership groups that can create regular celebrations will be more effective than those that limit themselves solely to control and command-models of working.

To be an optimistic leader does demand an inner sense of control and command. It is not an innate gift but a learned attitude based on discipline and awareness of one's own inner moods and emotional strategies. Two aspects of optimism need to be developed if leaders are to model a buoyant and cheerful approach to their work and relationships. The first is about the persistence of good or bad. People who are pessimistic tend to see bad events as normal and good events as lucky exceptions. They tend to use words like *all, always and never* as they look to the future in a negative way:

The unruly will **always** take control.
The new timetable system will **never** work.
All of the management team are incompetent.

In contrast, people who qualify these statements with other phrases such as *just lately, occasionally, some,* rather than *all* betray a more optimistic style of thinking that gives them increased buoyancy of spirit and an ability to spread joy:

It seems the unruly have taken control just **lately**.
Some aspects of the new timetable will not work.
Occasionally, some of the management may feel incompetent.

By ascribing permanence to the most negative aspects of experience, leaders can defend themselves against disappointment very effectively. However, they will not have the hope or the courage to invest in a future that they have already classified as a failure. By focusing on the permanence of the good and speaking positively about success and giftedness as a permanent disposition the leader can move people to greater optimism and joy in life. They can unlock gratitude and goodness and help them to grow in colleagues and young people:

You **always** do well in these meetings!
All your ideas seem to be fresh.
You **never** seem to lose your cool.

This way of speaking affirms a permanent disposition in others that allows them to claim and develop their gifts through encouragement. Similarly, in correcting others, the temporary status of their faults can be stressed. Then the one who is corrected is left with hope and the chance to grow, rather than receiving a vague and blanket condemnation of their behaviour:

Just lately you seem to have become lax in your record keeping.
Some aspects of your job do not seem to be working.
Occasionally you are in danger of letting the side down.

These qualifying phrases offer a clearer and more balanced picture of the person's work. It leaves them space for change and does not dampen their spirit unnecessarily. The language is clear when used in conversation with others but the language has most power in the self-talk we use in our own head and a healthy leader needs to listen to that inner-talk carefully, especially in a crisis situation.

How we think about the persistence of good or bad through time is one aspect of optimism. The second aspect is concerned with how far we allow good or bad to spread within our inner world. Some people have a tendency to contain the positive and be slow to express it, even to themselves. Others seem to contain the negative and do not let it spread through their work or relationships. Optimists tend to keep the negative contained in their minds as a one-off event that need not happen again. On the other hand, when something good happens they allow it space in their minds and share it with others according to their own personality. Optimists, faced with excellent results, will tend to share those results with others, return in their mind to the success and experience the glow that it brings. They are more likely to walk with a spring in their step and celebrate when they can. The joy they feel spreads out. In contrast, if the results are bad they will tend to contain the negative feelings by reminding themselves that the class was disruptive, the term was shorter, there was a large absenteeism and they had not focused on the needier pupils early enough. In other words they limited the feeling of failure to specific reasons which they could influence for future improvement.

In contrast, pessimists would allow the same failure to be generalised into a feeling that they are no good. That feeling would then touch their own self-worth and diminish self-esteem. They are then more likely to take that heaviness home to family and friends, kick the cat and drown their sorrows and return the next day confirmed in a sense of failure that is totally unjustified. The same pessimist, faced with successful results would limit the impact of the success by making it specific to the situation. They would see it as lucky, the test was too easy or anyone could have got that group through. Such an attitude limits joy and stops the party.

Cheerfulness

Optimism is therefore an inner attitude, a way of thinking and behaving that believes in goodness and expresses that goodness as the lasting element in experience. In the self-talk of leaders there is an inner world where love, faith and hope fight a spiritual battle against sadness and the brokenness of the human spirit. Optimism is a virtue that leaders need to cultivate as a source of joy and energy for their team. It is a choice made deep within, it creates the climate of the school or group in which they work. Optimism is a spiritual attitude that leads to life and the flourishing of each person in the community. Don Bosco made a unique link between spirituality and joy in his model of education; *Here we make holiness consist in being cheerful.*

For Don Bosco there was no such thing as a sad saint, or a good leader who never smiles or celebrates with others. He used to say that the devil was scared of cheerful people because he could not darken their spirit. Cheerfulness is another aspect of the asceticism of leadership that needs to be recognised by the leader as a spiritual gift that comes from optimism. It would be good for leaders to ask themselves what kind of presence they radiate into their community, what impact they have on the young people they serve and how they talk to themselves about their own performance. Such reflections will reveal that leaders are constantly making small acts of faith in the goodness of others, in their own goodness and integrity and the overwhelming goodness of God flowing through life and through human nature.

It is not possible to be authentically cheerful and happy without a peaceful heart. The absence of cheerfulness can be a sign that something needs to change. A reluctance to celebrate from time to time, a resistance to joy in others and a heaviness of spirit, point to the need to let go of some worry or guilt and perhaps talk to a friend or colleague. In other words, cheerfulness or its absence is an aspect of discernment for Christian leaders. When joy, optimism and cheerfulness have leaked away from the routine of work with the young and with colleagues, something needs to change. It is as if God is calling leaders back to themselves when they have strayed, like the Prodigal Son in the gospel, too far from their deepest source of life and energy. It was only when the prodigal son was brought to emptiness that he came to his senses. It was only when he remembered what he had lost that he was able to return to his father and to celebration and joy.

The path of leadership among the young is a sacred journey to spiritual maturity and to a deeper knowing of the spirit that moves in all people. The leader's road may twist and turn, it may go through many dark and threatening places and, at times, leave the leader alone and isolated. However, if leaders lose a sense of joy, cheerfulness and optimism for long periods then they may have wandered from that sacred path. They may need to be called back by the spirit in which they began their journey and the support and guidance of friends and colleagues along the way. The path of the leader is not easy; it is hidden in their heart and in the mind of God. Strewn along the way are opportunities for joy and celebration provided by friends, young people and by happy accidents. The good leader makes the most of these moments of joy and spreads them through the community and above all takes them to heart as gifts of God on the journey home to the Father.[20]

---

20 More detailed background on optimism is available in Martin Seligman's book *Authentic Happiness* listed in the resources section.

Questions

What aspects of your work give you hope and energy and how often do you think about those in an ordinary week?

What would you describe as your most successful experience in working with young people? What skills and gifts does that memory reveal in you as a leader and how often does it come to mind?

How often do you praise and encourage colleagues? How does praising others affect your own mood?

After a difficult time in work with young people, what helps you let go of the tiredness and tension and move your focus back towards the positive?

How many blessings have you experienced already today?

Reflection

Lord, there are so many reasons
To smile and be cheerful,
So many God-given moments
That are messengers of hope each day.

The inspiration of hard-working colleagues
The aroma of a good cup of coffee,
The chance to settle a difficult issue
Or the sound of the last school-bell of the day.

These opportunities for gratitude
Lie scattered through every day,
Seeding joy into greener pastures
Which revive my drooping spirit.

As a leader may I walk each day
With eyes open wide for goodness
Hidden in the honesty of a child,
The generosity of colleagues
And the inspiration of a new start.

Protect me Lord from the darker valleys
Of pessimism and complaint,
Where energy and direction are lost
In the shadow of self pity.

Give me instead the night-vision of a leader
To see through the darkened hearts of colleagues,
Towards the vision of a promised land,
Offering them the manna of encouragement
On the way to greener pastures.

Appendix 1

Reflection on RUAH

The word *Ruah* is used to describe the breath of God. The two syllables mimic the sound of breathing out and then in, of giving and receiving. The word reminds us of the need for life to flow rather than be forced. There are times when we need to give and times when we must receive. There are times when the focus needs to move out and times to move back to the centre. The act of breathing in and out reminds us of our connectedness and dependence, moment by moment, on the energy that sustains life. *Ruah* takes each person into the mystery of a shared life and away from that brittle independence that is celebrated so much in secular culture. Young people need to be reminded of this deeper spirit and their dependence on it if they are to escape the superficial culture that surrounds them in the imagined world of the media.

In Christian thinking, this breathing in and out of the spirit is an expression of God who always makes the first move, breathing out life. The story of Jesus, is God breathing into our lives to become one of us, in order for us, in our turn, to breathe in God's spirit and share it with each other. For Christian leaders, this is an invitation to make the first move in showing loving-kindness: initiating conversations, giving encouragement and offering forgiveness. The breath of the Spirit moves in every conversation and in each relationship. It connects us to an eternal moment in an ordinary event. All that needs to change is our own awareness that when we are moved to encourage, forgive, celebrate or suffer for the good of others; then the breath of God is moving within us. Spirituality and life-experience have entered an eternal embrace.

Respect

Respect means, literally to look at something again. It has come to mean the valuing of people and things and refraining from damaging or ignoring what is of value. For Christians, respect comes from a person's dignity as a child of God. Ungrateful and disobedient young people do not forfeit their dignity and need to be treated with respect. Even when they need to be disciplined, it must be done reasonably and with a calm and clear logic, rather than with an angry emotional outburst. Respect also implies the need for leadership to consult and take others' views into account in most situations. There is also a dimension of recognising effort and respecting the energy and commitment that individuals and groups bring to their work. Praise and encouragement, well-timed and specific, is a leadership gift that recognises the spirit in situations and celebrates it. Even the usual exchange of a smile or a *Hello* in a corridor is an expression of respect that resonates, in Christian communities, with an awareness of a spiritual reality. The holy ground of God's presence is the reality that gives eternal value to everything we do. Respect grows when the dignity of each person is guarded and celebrated in Christian schools and projects.

Understanding

To understand is to grasp the significance of something. To come to an understanding with someone is to have a clear and agreed way of working together. Both of these senses of the word are important in animating a community of Christians. To understand significance implies that a leader has time to reflect on events, accidents and opportunities. Patterns of behaviour, the success of projects, the mood of staff and the changing energy levels of a community all require understanding because they carry a lesson that might lead to a deeper wisdom. Understanding is not simply about the management of surface-events, but discerning the deeper currents of the spirit and the way that the spirit needs to be set free. Thinking-time and thoughtful conversations are central to the leader's role in understanding the community.

To come to an understanding with individuals and groups that is clear and reasonable is a vital strategy in leading with spirit. Understanding the limitations, thoughtlessness and immaturity of young people can help establish reasonable expectations that stretch their growth but never set them up to fail. Understanding colleagues and the particular pressures they carry can help a leader support and challenge more effectively.

Affection

As a style of leadership, animation depends upon the ability of the leader to express warmth and affection, even if they have hard decisions to make. The underlying logic of this aspect of leadership lies in the establishment of strong relationships that can survive the burden of bad news. If a person knows that the leader genuinely cares and appreciates them they are more likely to hear the invitations to growth and the criticisms that leader may offer. The leader who can move beyond the role to a relationship of affection will do more good and much less harm than the cold and distant managerial leader. The expression of warmth and affection is a long-term strategy, a daily drip-feed of conversation, affirmation and consultation that recognises the value of colleagues and young people. Only when people know that they are appreciated and recognised with affection will they reach deeper into their own spirit to find the energy for change and development. Another aspect of affective life that enhances leadership is the ability to express sorrow and vulnerability at the right time. A leader who is never wrong is not easy for colleagues to relate with. The ability to admit mistakes and ask forgiveness, models the value of relationships above efficiency in building community. Affection is not measurable, but it is part of the indispensable energy of the spirit that needs to be recognised in Christian community.

Humour

Leaders who maintain a constant smile fixed on their faces are seen as mad or just not realising where the problems are. The ability to relax, to laugh and smile, even at setbacks, can be a virtue in a leader. First of all, it can ease the panic in certain situations. It can open up a relaxed and more affectionate atmosphere. Humour can defuse tension in discipline situations and relieve the stress among colleagues. There is an energy liberated in genuine laughter that feeds the whole community. Such humour places people in the present moment, as a time to be celebrated and received as a gift. It connects with a deeper sense of shared life and togetherness and its absence for long periods is a sign that something is wrong in the community. With humour a community can also create celebrations, formal and informal that can move people off the agenda of targets and timetables to moments of gratitude and relaxation. The leader who never celebrates with individuals and groups will probably not be animating effectively.

The four animating attitudes as one

These four attitudes, taken together, amount to a faith journey for the leader. Each one is a gift and a challenge. For one leader, humour may come easily and yet affection may be difficult. For another leader, respect for individuals may be second-nature but expressing that respect, in affection, could be a challenge. In trying to live these values, leaders will find their own strengths confirmed and their weaknesses exposed. Hidden in the animator's skills is a pathway to spiritual growth, to fullness of life. The leader's vocation is both gift and challenge. All Christian vocations begin by affirming giftedness and then lead to growth through weakness. *We rise to heaven on the stepping-stones of our failures,* one Salesian priest wrote. The way of leadership is therefore a way of self-emptying and trust in the spirit that calls one to work with the young. These four attitudes are simply an illustration of that mystery at work in the lives of skilled professional leaders.

PRAYERS

Before giving a reprimand

Lord, give me courage to speak enough truth
Without judging the other person.
Help me to describe things accurately,
Without assigning motives that can only be guessed.
Above all, help me to listen carefully
To the other person's inner struggle,
Even as I focus on their behaviour.

Help me to know when to be quiet
And give me the right words to say,
And a stillness that allows me to hear
More than will be said in words.

Steady my purpose by good preparation,
Make me clear about the facts and the real issue,
Protect me from the anger and emotions
That may become focused upon me,
Guard my heart by your calming presence.

Whatever happens, keep me focused
On the goodness of the other person
And the needs of young people.

At a planning meeting

Lord of time and change,
Be with us as we explore the future.
May we be open to your spirit,
As a creative and energetic presence,
Moving in our ideas and in all our experience.

Give us patience with partial plans
And fragments of the future,
Glimpsed imperfectly in hopeful words.
Help us to sense your spirit,
Drawing us towards the future,
Even if it takes us away from comfortable patterns
And from our own pet projects.

Teach us to plan for a reality rooted in the gospel,
Rather than in our own needs.
Like humble servants of resources not our own,
May we be able to bring out of our hopes and experience
Things both old and new,
In the service of the young people of today.

As we build our plans,
Help us to remember that we are just servants
Of a community in which we are privileged to serve.
Open us up to the spirit
And to the task of building God's kingdom
In the hearts of young people, for a better world.

When Meeting Failure

The gospel demonstrates that failure is part of a process
Of coming to a richer and deeper place in life.
There is no growth without some breakdown,
No journey without a leaving behind
And nothing new without a change in patterns.

No real growth comes until something has fallen apart,
No flowers without seeds, no birth without pain,
No Resurrection without the shadow of the Cross,
Darkening and changing the status quo.

In the setback, with all its disappointment,
We touch again our own frailty
And the need for something more,
That draws us into God's mystery and purpose,
Unfolding towards an Easter yet to be revealed.

In recognising our shared shortcomings,
We plant our common roots
Into the earth of faith and friendship,
Recognising our weakness
And calling on a deeper spiritual energy
To open us to life and learning.

Thank you Lord, for the experience of failure,
For loving us even when we lose the plot
And stumble clumsily into life.
So guide us to the gift of life,
Wrapped up in this our failure.
Help us find a deeper strength
In your lasting love for losers.

Finding Thinking Time

Lord give me space
To see your face
In everything I do.
Help me sift significance
From all that I've been through.

Slow the pace of work awhile
And keep me still inside,
Until your patterns and your plans
Turn back work's anxious tide.

Help me mark with gratitude
All that has been achieved,
And count each blessing, large or small,
As your gift now revealed.

And as I count the hidden cost
Of working hard for youth,
Turn those costs to acts of faith,
On my journey home to you.

So give me time to count the ways
Your love has walked with me,
Through good and bad, in sad and glad,
Lord, set my spirit free.

After dealing with difficult youths

O Lord, I place into your hands
These needy damaged youths.
Give me wisdom and the time
To lead them towards life.

You did not crush the bruised reed,
Or quench a wavering flame.
Give me strength and hope to see
Your presence in their pain.

Not taking trouble home

Sometimes I am chilled to the bone
By troubles not my own.
They soak my mind and freeze my plans
And permeate my dreams.
Lord, lift the burden of these cares
And help me to let go
Of feeling too responsible
For all the things I know.

For a Prodigal Colleague

Lord, there are people at work,
Who are not pulling their weight,
Who do the minimum
With heartless efficiency.

It is so easy to write them off:
To blank them at meetings,
To look the other way on corridors,
Never look into their hearts.

Such people are part of salvation
For they reveal, by contrast,
The commitment of so many others
As a real blessing in community.

The prodigal son had a father
Who waited and hoped
For his son to come to his senses,
To a deeper sense of belonging.
Lord, as leaders, may we continue to hope,
Praying for the prodigals close to home,
For your spirit to move them
To share their gifts more generously.

Some Useful Books

Author	Date	Title	Publisher
Avalone P	1989	Reason, Religion and Kindness – The Educational Method of St John Bosco	New York, Don Bosco Publications
Best R	1996	Education Spirituality and The Whole Child	London, Cassell
Beuchner F	1982	The Sacred Journey	Harpercollins
Bishops Conference of England &Wales	1995	The Sign We Give	
Borgman D	2004	When Kumbaya is Not Enough	Massachusetts, Hendrickson
Copley T	2000	Spiritual Development in the State School	Exeter, Exeter University Press
Doyle M and Smith M	1999	Born and Bred? Leadership, Heart and Informal Education	London, YMCA
East T	2004	Effective Practices for Dynamic Youth Ministry	Winona, Saint Mary's Press
Eaude Tony	2006	Children's Spiritual, Moral, Social and Cultural Development	Exeter, Learning Matters
Gallagher J	2001	Soil for The Seed	Essex, McCrimmons
Gallagher J	2003	Serving The Young	Bolton, Don Bosco Publications
Gallagher M P	2003	Clashing Symbols	London, Darton Longman and Todd
Grace G	1995	School Leadership: Beyond Education Management	Falmer Press
Green M	2006	A Journey of Discovery: Spirituality and development in Youth Work	Leicester. National Youth Agency
Hardy A	1979	The Spiritual Nature of Man	Oxford, RERC
Hay D and Nye R	2006	The Spirit of The Child	London, Jessica Kingsley
James W	1902	The Varieties of Religious Experience	New York, Longmans

s W. Fowler	1999	Becoming Adult, Becoming Christian	Jossey Bass Wiley
erg L	1981	The Philosophy of Moral Development	San Francisco, Harper Row
y C	1992	Sponsoring Faith in Adolescence	Newtown Australia, EJ Dwyer
aerts H	1998	The Management & Leadership of Christian Schools	London Vllams Lasalliaaans Perspectif , Groot Bijgaarden,:246
mes	1995	Doing the Truth in Love	Paulist Press International
thy R(Ed)	2005	The Vision of Catholic Youth Ministry	Winona, Saint Mary's Press
ey D	2001	Ordinary Ways	Bolton, Don Bosco Publications
ey D	2003	Via Lucis	Bolton, Don Bosco Publications
	1950	The Idea of The Holy	Oxford, University Press
r A and v G	2001	A Qualitative Exploration of Relational Consciousness	International Journal of Children's Spirituality Vol 6
son E	1996	The Original Vision	RERC, Oxford
nan	2004	Authentic Happiness	London, Nicholas Brealey
N	1997	Dimensions of The Sacred	London, Fontana
d L & Juliano C	2002	Collaboration: Uniting Our Gifts in Ministry	Ave Maria Press
ner A	1999	Spirituality and The Curriculum	London, Cassell
P	2002	Liquid Church	Carlisle, Paternoster Press
F, Nye R, e S	2002	Psychology for Christian Ministry	London, Routledge
anley M	2002	Don Bosco's Gospel Way	Bolton, Don Bosco Publications
A	1998	Spiritual Pedagogy	Oxford, Cullham College

Some Web-Based Resources

Bloxham Project	A site that explores the un-measurable and spiritual aspects of education	www.bloxhamproject.org.uk/
CAFOD	Has an excellent worship database on Justice and Peace	http://www.cafod.org.uk/resources/worship
CASE	Provides a good range of resources and downloads	http://www.caseresources.org.uk
CES	The Catholic Education Service provides background on Evangelisation, National Projects and many useful links	http://www.cesew.org.uk
CNRS	The Catholic Network for Retreats and Spirituality	http://cnrs.retreats.org.uk/
Culham	An Anglican based support service for Religious Education, excellent links and resources	http://www.culham.ac.uk/
CYS	Provides a range of support for informal Church work with youth	www.catholicyouthservices.org.uk/
De La Salle	A daily prayer source for schools and youth groups	http://www.prayingeachday.org/
Faceup	An online magazine for 14-18s who think a little deeper	http://faceup.ie/
Infed	Informal Education is the focus of this site that links leadership and spirituality	http://www.infed.org/
NYA	Has a downloadable version of *A Journey of Discovery* listed in the bibliography	http://www.nya.org.uk/
RE Online	A hub site for a wide range of faith based resources for all ages	http://www.reonline.org.uk/
SDB	A school chaplaincy web site offering current ideas from Thornleigh College Bolton	http://www.salesians.org.uk/chap/
Search	The Search Institute referred to in the text offers an holistic community approach to nurturing the young	http://www.search-institute.org/
Youth Work	Ideas, magazine and resources for Christian youth ministry	ttp://www.youthwork.co.uk/